U·X·L newsmakers

10/05

U·X·L newsmakers

volume **1** one

A–Fe

Judy Galens,
Kelle S. Sisung

Carol Brennan, *Contributing Writer*

Jennifer York Stock, *Project Editor*

U·X·L
An imprint of Thomson Gale,
a part of The Thomson Corporation

REF
920
GAL

THOMSON
™
GALE

Detroit • New York • San Francisco • San Diego • New Haven, Conn. • Waterville, Maine • London • Munich

U•X•L Newsmakers

Judy Galens, Kelle S. Sisung, and Carol Brennan

Project Editor
Jennifer York Stock

Editorial
Michael D. Lesniak, Allison McNeill

Rights Acquisition and Management
Peggie Ashlevitz, Edna Hedblad, Sue Rudolph

Imaging and Multimedia
Lezlie Light, Mike Logusz, Denay Wilding

Product Design
Kate Scheible

Composition
Evi Seoud

Manufacturing
Rita Wimberly

LIBRARY OF CONGRESS CATALOGING-IN-PUBLICATION DATA

Galens, Judy, 1968-

UXL newsmakers / Judy Galens and Kelle S. Sisung ; Allison McNeill, project editor.

   p. cm.

   Includes bibliographical references and index.

   ISBN 0-7876-9189-5 (set) — ISBN 0-7876-9190-9 (v. 1)—ISBN 0-7876-9191-7 (v. 2)—ISBN 0-7876-9194-1 (v. 3)—ISBN 0-7876-9195-X (v. 4)

     1. Biography—20th century—Dictionaries, Juvenile. 2. Biography—21st century—Dictionaries, Juvenile. 3. Celebrities—Biography—Dictionaries, Juvenile. I. Sisung, Kelle S. II. McNeill, Allison. III. Title.

CT120.G26 2004
920′.009′051—dc22

             2004009426

contents

volume **1** one

 contents

 volume **2** two

volume **3** three

 contents

volume **4** four

Italic type *indicates volume number.*

Entertainment

Government

Music

Science

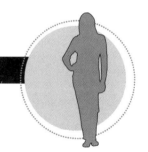

Social Issues

Sports

Writing

U•*X•L Newsmakers* is the place to turn for information on personalities active on the current scene. Containing one hundred biographies, *U•X•L Newsmakers* covers contemporary figures who are making headlines in a variety of fields, including entertainment, government, literature, music, pop culture, science, and sports. Subjects include international figures, as well as people of diverse ethnic backgrounds.

Format

Biographies are arranged alphabetically across four volumes. Each entry opens with the individual's birth date, place of birth, and field of endeavor. Entries provide readers with information on the early life, influences, and career of the individual or group being profiled. Most entries feature one or more photographs of the subject, and all entries provide a list of sources for further reading about the individual or group. Readers may also locate entries by using the Field of Endeavor table of contents listed in the front of each volume, which lists biographees by vocation.

Features

- A Field of Endeavor table of contents, found at the front of each volume, allows readers to access the biographees by the category for which they are best known. Categories include: Art/Design, Business, Entertainment, Government, Music, Science, Social Issues, Sports, and Writing. When applicable, subjects are listed under more than one category for even greater access.

- Sidebars include information relating to the biographee's career and activities (for example, writings, awards, life milestones), brief biographies of related individuals, and explanations of movements, groups, and more, connected with the person.

- Quotes from and about the biographee offer insight into their lives and personal philosophies.

- More than 180 black-and-white photographs are featured across the volumes.

- Sources for further reading, including books, magazine articles, and Web sites, are provided at the end of each entry.

- A general index, found at the back of each volume, quickly points readers to the people and subjects discussed in *U•X•L Newsmakers*.

Comments and Suggestions

The individuals chosen for these volumes were drawn from all walks of life and from across a variety of professions. Many names came directly from the headlines of the day, while others were selected with the interests of students in mind. By no means is the list exhaustive. We welcome your suggestions for subjects to be profiled in future volumes of *U•X•L Newsmakers* as well as comments on this work itself. Please write: Editor, *U•X•L Newsmakers,* U•X•L, 27500 Drake Road, Farmington Hills, Michigan 48331-3535; call toll-free: 1-800-877-4253; or send an e-mail via www.gale.com.

U·X·L newsmakers

Freddy Adu

June 2, 1989 • Tema, Ghana

Soccer player

Freddy Adu is like any average teenager. He goofs around with his friends, enjoys going to the movies, loves PlayStation, and hates doing his homework. Unlike most kids, however, he earns about $500,000 a year. Adu's hefty paycheck comes from playing soccer. In November of 2003, when he signed with Major League Soccer (MLS), Adu became the youngest person to play for a professional American sports league since 1877. Called "the boy with the magic feet," all eyes are on the young superstar who many predict will make soccer the new favorite American pastime.

The playing fields of Ghana

Freddy Adu is so gifted and seems so mature that people question whether he could actually be as young as he is. According to his birth certificate, however, he was born on June 2, 1989, in the seaport town of Tema, Ghana, in West Africa. Tema is known for two things: fishing and soccer. Adu was kicking a soccer ball by the time he was two-

and-a-half years old. By the age of six, while father Maxwell and mother Emelia ran a local convenience store, he was playing in barefoot pick-up games with boys two or three times his own age. "I did not go one day without playing," Adu told Leslie Stahl in a 2003 *60 Minutes* interview. "It was just kicking and learning."

In 1997, when Adu was eight, his parents participated in an immigration lottery through the U.S. embassy in Ghana. According to Emelia Adu, the reason was to give her children, Freddy and younger brother Fredua, the chance for a better education. The Adus won the lottery and all four packed up and moved to the United States, settling in Potomac, Maryland, near Washington, D.C. Shortly after arriving in America, Maxwell Adu abandoned his family. To support the boys, Emelia took on two jobs, getting up at five A.M. every morning and working more than seventy hours a week.

> **"When I'm out there on the field, I'm in a whole different world."**

Naturally, Freddy Adu turned to soccer, playing with other children at his school playground. His fourth-grade friends were amazed, and one of them invited him to play in a tournament hosted by the Potomac Soccer Association. It was his first time playing in an organized soccer event. Adu dazzled everyone, but was particularly noticed by financial consultant Arnold Tarzy, who was also the coach of the Cougars, a Potomac soccer team. Adu left such an impression on Tarzy that the Cougars coach tracked him down, and within forty-eight hours of the tournament Adu had joined his team. Tarzy became Adu's supporter and friend as well as his coach.

The buzz starts

When Adu was ten, Tarzy suggested that he travel to Italy with a U.S. Olympic Development Program team to compete in a youth tournament for players under age fourteen. Adu's team not only won the

Learning the Language

According to sportswriter Rick Reilly, Freddy Adu "can do things with a soccer ball that make you wonder if it's not Velcroed to his feet." At a very young age Adu mastered dribbling and passing. He also tackled the most complicated of soccer moves. Several of these moves are named after the soccer players who made the moves famous. Perhaps one day young soccer players will be learning "The Adu," but in the meantime, here are some of the moves that Freddy uses to score on the soccer field.

- *Beckham.* Named for David Beckham (1975–) from England. The move is used to get a special spin, or "bend," on a ball as it is kicked toward the goal. A player uses the side of his foot to slice under the ball, at the same time leaning back as far as he can to get the most lift. The

Beckham was popularized in the 2002 movie *Bend it Like Beckham,* about a young Indian girl who struggles to pursue her dream of being a soccer star like her idol, David Beckham.

- *Cruyff.* Named for Johan Cruyff (1947–) from the Netherlands. A player pretends to be kicking the ball with the inside of his right foot, but instead shifts his weight to the left foot, turns his right foot to point down, and switches the ball to his left foot. The move is used to "fake out" opponents.

- *Maradona.* Named for Diego Maradona (c. 1961–) from Argentina. The move consists of stopping the ball with one foot while making a 180-degree turn above it. It is used to control the ball and change direction.

competition, but Adu scored more points than anyone in the tournament and was named Most Valuable Player (MVP). The soccer world stood up and took notice. Adu was younger by several years than most of the players. In addition, he was pitted against players from Europe, where soccer (known as football) is king and people train seriously from a very young age. Major European teams such as Inter Milan (considered to be the New York Yankees of soccer) came calling, hoping to lure Adu to Europe.

During the following year Adu also attracted attention from the U.S. Soccer Federation and from companies such as Adidas, who were eager to have the soccer star with the megawatt smile promote their products. But Adu's mother said no. "He's too young," Emelia Adu told Amy Rosewater of *USA Today* in 2001. "I want him to get an education." Emelia Adu struggled with her decision, but felt she was making the right choice for her son.

Freddy's skills were not limited to the soccer field. He was also a budding artist. In his first art competition, which he entered in the fifth grade, Adu won the top prize in the county. He was also an exceptional student. Shortly after joining the Cougars, Adu received a full scholarship to attend The Heights, a prestigious boys' school in Potomac. He did so well that he skipped the seventh grade. Adu also played basketball, scoring twenty-eight points in his first junior varsity game.

But Adu's soccer ability was too bright to hide, and coaches continued to knock on his door. In 2001 John Ellinger, coach of the U.S. Soccer Federation's Under-17 team, asked Adu to attend a weekend tournament in Florida. After watching Adu's performance, Ellinger told Mark Starr in a *Newsweek* interview, "I see him do things I haven't seen the pros do." He described one move in particular: "The kid fielded a pass on the outside of his left foot, flicked it up and over his head—and over the defender—and corralled the ball without breaking stride."

Ellinger invited Adu to train at the federation's Soccer Academy, which is part of the IMG Academies in Bradenton, Florida. Run by the sports agency IMG, the 190-acre campus is an elite training ground for top athletes in a variety of sports. For example, only thirty of the nation's best young players are invited to attend the soccer academy. In 2002 Adu's mother agreed to let him go, and he moved to Florida, becoming, at twelve, the youngest member of America's Under-17 soccer team.

Fancy footwork

Adu did not disappoint his coaches in Bradenton. He consistently scored high in matches against other youth squads, as well as in exhibition games against several college and professional teams. In March of 2003, just weeks after he became a U.S. citizen, Adu helped his team qualify for the Under-17 World Championships. In August he and his American teammates traveled to Finland for the finals. Adu scored four goals in two games, one a critical semifinal match against South Korea. Although his team ultimately lost to Brazil, the word was out that Adu was the kid to watch. In fact, according to one scout quoted in a March 2003 *Sports Illustrated* article, "He's going to be the best player in the world someday."

Coaches and leagues were again pounding at the door; there were even some tempting offers for Adu to train in Europe. It was

The Next Pelé?

Young Freddy Adu has often been compared to Pelé, considered by many to be the most famous, and perhaps the greatest, soccer player of all time. Edson Arantes do Nascimento was born in 1940 in Tres Coracoes, Brazil, the son of a soccer player. He turned pro at age sixteen and played for the Santos Football Club in Brazil from 1956 to 1974. In 1975, in an attempt to boost the sport of soccer in the United States, Pelé was signed to play with the New York Cosmos of the North American Soccer League. He played with the team for two years before retiring in 1977. Throughout his career, Pelé scored an amazing 1,280 goals in 1,362 professional games. He also holds the record as the only team player to win three World Cup titles. People were amazed by Pelé's skill on the soccer field, but they were also captivated by his charming personality and winning smile.

After retiring, Pelé continued to be active, serving as a sports commentator and traveling around the world as a soccer ambassador. In 1997 he was elected minister of sports in Brazil. In 2004 he appeared in Freddy Adu's first television commercial, for Pepsi's Sierra Mist. In his interview with Leslie Stahl, Adu relayed the advice Pelé gave him: "He told me to keep my head up and just play."

reported that he was offered $3 million from England's Manchester United. Adu turned them all down. For one thing, the Adus did not need the money, since Freddy had recently signed a $1 million contract with Nike to endorse their sports line. In addition, Adu was itching to play with the pros. According to European Federation rules, any player transferring from outside the European Union is limited to playing in youth leagues until he or she turns eighteen. "If you're good enough," Adu remarked to Stahl, "you're old enough.'

So, when America's Major League Soccer (MLS) came knocking, Adu answered. In November of 2003, he signed on with the MLS and was offered a four-year contract with a two-year league option. In January of 2004 he was snatched up by D.C. United to play professional soccer. His yearly salary: a cool $500,000, which is almost twice that of the average American soccer player. Adu was fourteen years old; the typical age of a professional soccer player is twenty-seven.

Freddy's future

Adu missed most of D.C. United's training camp in early 2004 because he was still in school. Thanks to his high grades (he consis-

Freddy Adu warms up before a 2004 game against the Los Angeles Galaxy. AP/Wide World Photos. Reproduced by permission.

tently earned straight A's) and the Soccer Federation's accelerated academic program, he graduated from high school in March, three years ahead of schedule. He then moved back to Maryland to live with his mother, who will drive him to and from practice. The Adus live in a brand new house purchased by Freddy, and Emelia Adu has finally been able to quit her job. "She doesn't work anymore. She's done," Adu told Stahl. "You know she's worked so hard." Emelia Adu has not forgotten, however, that Freddy is still a boy. She expects him to do the usual chores that every kid does, such as mowing the lawn, doing the dishes, and vacuuming.

Adu, however, is not a normal boy. On April 3, 2004, when he took the field for his first professional match, millions of people tuned in to watch the fourteen-year-old on *ABC Sports*. The match between D.C. United and the San Jose Earthquakes was the MLS season opener and had been sold out for months. Fans swarmed the stands, chanting "Freddy, Freddy," until finally, during the second half of the game, Adu was brought in. The 5-foot-8-inch forward, however, made a very low key showing. In fact, he never even attempted to score a goal. Adu's coaches were not worried, chalking up his lackluster play to all the media frenzy. Adu himself seemed unfazed about his performance, commenting to sportswriter Joseph White on the FOXSportsworld Web site, "I got it out of the way, and now I'm ready to go.... I'm glad it's over."

Adu's next goal is to play on the U.S. team in the 2006 World Cup. Teams representing individual countries compete every four years for the world championship of soccer. Until then, hopes are high that Adu will spark the interest in soccer in America that is shared by the rest of the world. Although many children play the game in school, not much attention is paid to the sport at the professional level. Discussing Adu in a November 2003 *Sports Illustrated* article, MLS commissioner Don Garber commented, "It's not just about performing on the field. It's about being a founding father of the sport for a generation."

In the midst of all the hype, however, Adu, has remained a down-to-earth young man. In a press conference held just before his professional debut and reported on the *Sports Illustrated* Web site, he focused on the upcoming game and his team: "I'm not coming out here to become the savior of American soccer. I'm anxious to get out there and play and have fun because when I'm on the soccer field that's when I'm at my happiest."

For More Information

Periodicals

Reilly, Rick. "Ready Freddy." *Sports Illustrated* (December 1, 2003): p. 94.

Rosewater, Amy. "Soccer Prodigy Adu Won't Go to Highest Bidder." *USA Today* (August 23, 2001): p. 23.

Starr, Mark. "A Strong Kick for American Soccer." *Newsweek* (December 30, 2002): p. 70.

Wahl, Grant. "Freddy Adu: At 13, America's Greatest Soccer Prodigy Has the World at His Feet." *Sports Illustrated* (March 3, 2003): pp. 40–49.

Wahl, Grant. "Freddy Stays." *Sports Illustrated* (November 24, 2003): p. 24.

Web Sites

Stahl, Leslie. "Just Going Out to Play: Interview with Freddy Adu." *60 Minutes* (March 28, 2004). *CBSNews.com.* http://www.cbsnews.com/ stories/2004/03/25/60minutes/main608681.shtml (accessed on March 31, 2004).

"Adu in Demand: Everyone Has Advice For 14-Year-Old as MLS Debut Nears." *SI.com: Sports Illustrated.* http://sportsillustrated.cnn.com/ 2004/soccer/03/28/bc.sport.soccer.adu (accessed on March 31, 2004).

"Freddy Adu Says Hello." *CBSNews.com.* http://www.cbsnews.com/stories/ 2003/11/20/national/main584743.shtml (accessed on March 31, 2004).

White, Joseph. "Adu Makes MLS Debut in D.C.'s 2–1 Win Over San Jose." *FOXSportsworld.com.* http://www.foxsportsworld.com/content/view? contentId=2290392 (accessed on April 4, 2004).

Anthony Anderson

August 15, 1970 • Augusta, Maine

Actor, writer, producer

With his boyish face and gap-toothed smile, and weighing over 270 pounds, Anthony Anderson is not a typical Hollywood leading man. In fact, for most of his career he has played second banana in such films as *Big Momma's House* (2000), *Barbershop* (2002), and *Kangaroo Jack* (2003). In March of 2003, however, Anderson signed a deal with the Warner Brothers Network to write, produce, and star in his own TV sitcom, *All About the Andersons.* And in 2004 he finally came into his own, appearing in at least four major movies. In fact, most moviegoers couldn't turn around without seeing Anderson grinning down from the screen. In an interview with Anderson on the *Filmcritic* Web site, Sean O'Connell remarked, "Few could argue with the fact that Anderson is the hardest working young talent in show business."

Born into the business

Anthony Anderson was born on August 15, 1970, in Augusta, Maine, but was raised in Compton, California, a suburb of Los Angeles. His mother, Dora, was a movie extra, so young Anthony literally grew up on film sets. By the age of five, Anderson followed in his mother's footsteps and began appearing in television commercials. He showed such promise as an actor that he attended a Los Angeles performing arts high school, where he won an award given by the Afro-Academic, Cultural, Technological and Scientific Olympics (ACT-SO), a program sponsored by the National Association for the Advancement of Colored People (NAACP). The annual award recognizes students in grades nine through twelve "who exemplify scholastic and cultural excellence."

Anderson won the ACT-SO award for a monologue, or short speech, which he performed from the play *The Great White Hope* (1968), written by American playwright Howard Sackler (1929–1982). The play is based on the life of Jack Johnson (1878–1946),

> **"This is what my energy was created to do— entertain, to have an effect on people's lives with my work."**

the first African American heavyweight-boxing champion. Jackson was portrayed by James Earl Jones (1931–) both on the stage and in the film version of the play. Anderson considers Jones to be his favorite actor, and credits him as his inspiration. "I really respect and admire his work," Anderson commented to O'Connell. "It's why I do what I do."

As a result of his talent, Anderson earned a drama scholarship to attend Howard University, a prestigious African American college in Washington, D.C. It was also a result of Anderson's determination and drive, since life could have been quite different for a child raised in Compton. The suburb is known for its gang violence, and frequently makes the news for incidents of drive-by shootings and drug arrests. In a 2002 interview appearing on the *Femail* magazine Web site, Anderson commented, "You were either made a ward of the court, on parole, or dead at 21 if you grew up in Compton, Los Angeles."

Stepping stones

After graduating from Howard, Anderson paid the usual dues of an actor, taking such bit parts as that of Alley Hood #2 in the 1996 television movie *Alien Avengers*. His work on *Avengers* helped land him his first major job, as a regular on the NBC morning teen sitcom *Hang Time*. From 1996 to 1998 Anderson played the role of Teddy Brodis, a bumbling high school basketball player. He was in his mid-twenties at the time, but with his baby face and knack for comedy, no one would have guessed it. During his *Hang Time* days, Anderson also popped up on other television shows, including *In the House*, which starred rapper LL Cool J (1968–), and on *NYPD Blue*.

In 1999 Anderson made the leap to the big screen in the 1930s prison comedy *Life,* playing opposite established stars Eddie Murphy (1961–) and Martin Lawrence (1965–). That same year he also appeared in director Barry Levinson's 1950s coming-of-age movie *Liberty Heights*. In 2000 Anderson had what many consider to be his breakthrough year, when he played opposite Martin Lawrence in the hit comedy *Big Momma's House*. He also appeared in *Me, Myself, and Irene,* which starred Jim Carrey (1962–), one of Hollywood's biggest box office draws. Critics claimed it was a forgettable Carrey film, but Anderson, as Carrey's son, Jamaal, drew rave reviews.

Not all of Anderson's movies were comedies. Some were dramas, like *Kingdom Come* (2001). Some were action films such as *Romeo Must Die* (2000) and *Cradle 2 the Grave* (2003), both starring Jet Li (1963–), and *Exit Wounds* (2001), a Steven Seagal (1951–) thriller. In these films Anderson usually provided the comic relief, and he was consistently singled out over the stars with bigger billing. For example, in *Cradle,* many reviewers felt that as Tommy, the wise-cracking henchman, Anderson's acting stole the show.

All about Anthony

Anderson was on a career roll, starring in at least four movies each year, beginning in 2000. The exception was 2002, when his only on-screen performance was in *Barbershop*. He also continued to do guest spots on television programs, including *Ally McBeal* and *My Wife and Kids*. It seemed that Anderson was everywhere and could do anything,

Anthony Anderson at the Movies

Life (1999).

Liberty Heights (1999).

Urban Legends: Final Cut (2000).

Romeo Must Die (2000).

Me, Myself, and Irene (2000).

Big Momma's House (2000).

3 Strikes (2000).

Two Can Play at That Game (2001).

See Spot Run (2001).

Kingdom Come (2001).

Exit Wounds (2001).

Barbershop (2002).

Scary Movie 3 (2003).

Malibu's Most Wanted (2003).

Kangaroo Jack (2003).

Cradle 2 the Grave (2003).

My Baby's Daddy (2004).

Agent Cody Banks 2: Destination London (2004).

Harold and Kumar Go to White Castle (2004).

All American Game (2004).

King's Ransom (2005).

but he was not yet a household name. In 2003 all that changed. Anderson had a blockbuster hit with the film *Kangaroo Jack,* and then bounced back to the small screen in a big way to write, produce, and star in his own television sitcom.

For several years Anderson had been toying with the idea of writing a television script. In March of 2003 he finally pitched his idea to Warner Brothers (WB) executives, and they loved it. Mike Clements, a WB senior vice president of development, told Leslie Ryan of *Television Week* that Anderson "is such an enthusiastic and energetic guy that when he was telling us these stories, well, we literally hadn't laughed like that in a really long time."

Clements also commented that the stories were so outrageous they had to be true. And, in fact, they are. *All About the Andersons* is about a struggling actor (played by Anderson) who, along with his young son, moves back home to live with his parents. Anderson based the idea on a period in his own life when he moved back home after graduating from college. Still jobless, he just sat around the house eating. Eventually he drove his parents crazy. His stepfather was so determined to get Anderson out of the house that he put a padlock on the refrigerator, took out all the phone jacks and installed a pay phone, and bought a coin-operated washer and dryer so that Anderson was forced to pay in order to wash his clothes.

Anderson knew these things were a bit abnormal, but he also knew they were funny. "I realized my family was funny, because nobody ever wanted to leave our house," he explained in *People.* After his show debuted in the fall of 2003, TV viewers were given a glimpse into Anderson's early life, and they agreed with him: his family was hilarious. Critics, however, wrote mixed reviews. In particular, some felt that the relationship between Anderson's character and his on-screen father, played by veteran actor John Amos (1941–), was sometimes a bit harsh for a family comedy. In general, though, Anderson received applause for his acting and most agreed that *All About the Andersons* showed great potential. However, the show was cancelled in April of 2004.

A long way from Compton

In 2004 Anderson continued juggling his time between TV and film. He costarred in several movies, including *Agent Cody Banks 2* with teen actor Frankie Muniz (1985–). In *Agent Cody* he played Derek, the wisecracking handler of the young secret agent. He also finished work on *King's Ransom,* the first movie in which Anderson took top billing. It seemed that the big man with the big potential was finally coming into his own.

What are his future plans? Although he admitted in *People* that "comedy is second nature for me," Anderson has also noted that he is eager to take on more dramatic roles. He also plans to balance out his movie choices by appearing in some movies that are family friendly and some that are more edgy. He explained to Julia Roman on the *Latino Review* Web site, "It's good making films that my family can sit back and enjoy." Anderson and his wife, Alvina, who was his college sweetheart, have two children, Kyra and Nathan.

Anderson also has plans to act on the stage, and hopes one day to do some stand-up comedy. The multitalented actor has come a long way from Compton, and there seems to be no stopping him. As busy as he is, Anderson frequently takes time out to visit his old school and talk to kids about what they can accomplish. As reported on the *Femail* Web site, he has urged young people to "set your seights on more than what you see around you, see beyond." Better than the message is Anderson himself, who is living proof that big dreams can become a reality.

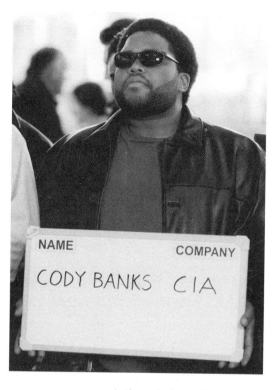

Anthony Anderson in movie still from Agent Cody Banks 2 *(2004).*
© MGM Pictures/Zuma/Corbis.

For More Information

Periodicals

Kelleher, Terry. "All About the Andersons." *People* (October 27, 2003): p. 36.

Ryan, Leslie. "The Gonzo Life of Mr. Anderson." *Television Week* (April 28, 2003): p. 10.

Speier, Michael. "All About the Andersons." *Daily Variety* (September 10, 2003): pp. 50–51.

Web Sites

"Anthony Anderson Interview." *Femail.com.* http://www.femail.com.au/ma_anthonyanderson.htm (accessed on April 1, 2004).

"ACT-SO." *NAACP.org.* http://www.naacp.org/work/actso/act-so.shtml (accessed on April 2, 2004).

O'Connell, Sean. "Grave Discussions: Talking With Anthony Anderson." *Filmcritic.com.* http://www.filmcritic.com/misc/emporium.nsf/0/b130b479fe49434108256ccb0019880b?OpenDocument (accessed on April 1, 2004).

Roman, Julia. "My Baby's Daddy: Interview With Anthony Anderson." *Latino Review.* http://www.latinoreview.com/films_2004/miramax/mydaddysbaby/anthony-interview.html (accessed on April 2, 2004).

Avi Arad

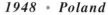

U·X·L newsmakers • volume 1

1948 • Poland

Producer, executive, toy designer

Avi Arad may have the coolest job in the world, considering that he gets to hang around with the likes of Spider-Man, the Incredible Hulk, and the Fantastic Four. As chief creative officer (CCO) of Marvel Enterprises, Arad has a hand in all areas of the superhero business, from developing and marketing toys to publishing comic books. He is also president and chief executive officer (CEO) of Marvel Studios, which means that it is Arad's job to oversee the process that takes Marvel superheroes from the comic book page to the silver screen. Arad should be busy for a very long time, since Marvel has about 2,700 characters just waiting to burst onto the movie scene. Arad, as their biggest fan, is only too happy to provide some super-human assistance.

Comic book escape

Avi Arad was born in Poland, but soon after his birth his parents took their young son to live in Israel. The year was 1948, and many people living in Eastern Europe were looking for a way to make a better life after the devastation of World War II (1939–45). While growing up, Arad's passion was reading, and he described his favorite childhood pastime in a 2003 interview with Scott Bowles on the *USA Today* Web site. "We didn't have much back then," Arad explained. "Maybe I just wanted to escape that life into something more fantastic." As a result, Arad devoured comic books such as *Superman* and *Spider-Man,* which were translated into Hebrew.

In 1965, when he was seventeen years old, Arad joined the Israeli army, called the Israel Defense Forces. Israeli citizens are required to serve in their military, and most do it willingly because

> **"I believe that comic books are as valid a form of literature as any other."**

they feel they have an obligation to protect their country. In 1967 Arad was wounded and spent the next fifteen months recuperating in a hospital. After he left the army he immigrated to the United States, where he attended college at Hofstra University in New York. He paid for his education by teaching Hebrew and working as a truck driver.

After graduating from college, Arad began working in the toy business, a career that he would devote himself to for the rest of his life. He started out as a toy designer, creating products for almost every major toy company in the United States, including Hasbro, Mattell, and Tyco. Throughout his career it is estimated that he designed more than 150 toys and games. In the late 1980s he permanently joined forces with Toy Biz, which was owned by fellow Israeli immigrant Isaac "Ike" Perlmutter (1945–). At Toy Biz, Arad was responsible for developing such memorable toys as My Pretty Ballerina, Magic Bottle Baby, and Baby Wanna Talk. He also created a series of X-Men action figures that were gobbled up by kids of all ages, bringing in more than $30 million dollars for the company.

The story of Marvel

In 1993 Toy Biz struck an agreement with Marvel Entertainment to manufacture toys based on Marvel comic book characters. In exchange Marvel received a substantial piece of Toy Biz. From then on, the story of Avi Arad became linked with the story of Marvel. Marvel Comics was founded by publisher Martin Goodman (1908–1992). In 1939 Goodman began selling comic books for ten cents an issue. A comic book is a magazine that consists of a series of panels used to tell a story. Each panel contains a brightly colored picture, and often some text. Because comic books were inexpensive to produce and the action-packed stories were so popular, especially with young people, Goodman became the father of a very successful industry.

Throughout the years Marvel hit highs and lows, but it steadily built a fan base of comic book readers who were fiercely loyal to their favorite comic book characters. By the 1960s the company was selling fifty million comic books a year, and superheroes like the Incredible Hulk were everywhere, appearing not only in comic books but on T-shirts, lunch boxes, and Saturday morning cartoons. Over the years Marvel also changed hands a number of times. In 1988 the company was purchased by the Andrews Group, which changed its name to Marvel Entertainment and put finance guru Ronald Perelman (1943–) in charge.

Perelman had extensive business experience, but no experience in the comic book business. He expanded the company into other areas such as sports trading cards, and took out loans that the company was unable to repay. Arad and Perlmutter tried to advise Perelman that he was sitting on a gold mine, and that Marvel characters had the potential to be marketed in many ways. Perelman refused to listen, and by 1996 Marvel was filing for bankruptcy and heading for failure.

After a major court battle, Perelman lost control of the company. After all the dust settled, Toy Biz took over Marvel in 1998, and Arad and Perlmutter were in the driver's seat. They changed the company name to Marvel Enterprises and divided it into three divisions: toys, entertainment and licensing, and comic book publishing. Toy Biz designs, develops, markets, and distributes toys; Marvel Studios creates movies, video games, and television programs featuring Marvel characters; and the publishing division focuses on the core product that Marvel has always produced—comic books.

The History of Spidey

Spider-Man was the brainchild of legendary comic book writer Stan Lee (1922–), who joined Marvel Comics when he was only sixteen years old. Lee is often credited with revolutionizing the comic book industry. The character of Spider-Man first appeared in 1962 as part of the comic book series "Amazing Fantasy." He became so popular that the series was renamed *Amazing Spider-Man.* In 1977 Spider-Man began starring in his own comic strip, which eventually appeared in more than five hundred newspapers around the world. Lee wrote and edited the strip, which appeared seven days a week, while Fred Kids drew the panels. In the late 1980s, Lee's younger brother, Larry Lieber, became Spider-Man's artist.

The first Spider-Man animated television series was launched on ABC in 1967, and ran for two seasons. The first live-action program aired on CBS from 1977 to 1979. Since then Spidey has made regular appearances on the small screen. He returned in his own animated series in 1981 and was joined by several super pals, including the Incredible Hulk, in *Spider-Man and His Amazing Friends,* which aired on NBC from 1982 to 1985. In the 1990s and 2000s, Spider-Man starred in several successful series that were aired on major networks, including MTV.

With the release of the *Spider-Man* movie in 2002, a whole new generation of fans was introduced to the web-slinging hero. He also swings into action on countless video games, and there is even a Spider-Man ride on the Marvel Super Hero Island at the Universal Studios theme park in Orlando, Florida.

Part of Spider-Man's popularity seems to be that Lee created a superhero who is also very human. Peter Parker was an ordinary student until he was bitten by a radioactive spider while attending a science demonstration. The bite gave him amazing powers, including super strength, a sixth "spider" sense that allowed him to detect danger, and the ability to stick to walls and ceilings. He was also able to spin and shoot webs, thanks to a webshooter of his own design. Parker has used his spider powers against such villains as Cyclone, Doc Ock, and the Kingpin.

Regardless of his amazing abilities, however, Parker is an average Joe. He is of average height at 5-foot 10 inches, average weight at 165 pounds, and has average hair color (brown). He also worries about everyday things like money, girlfriends, and dandruff. Basically, underneath the mask, Spider-Man is a hero that everyone can relate to. And he continues to be one of the most well-known and popular Marvel characters of all time.

Marvel revived

Perlmutter, the more conservative half of the duo, became the numbers man who handled the business end of things. Arad became the creative force behind the company. And according to many, it is Arad who deserves the credit for Marvel's meteoric comeback. Since 1998 the company's stock has risen 136 percent and, as it did in its heyday, Marvel dominates the comic book industry. Why is Arad given all the credit? According to Dan Raviv, author of *Comic Wars,* "The key to

Marvel's current success is that Avi Arad loves the Marvel heroes. He knows their stories backwards and forwards."

As the company's chief creative officer (CCO), Arad has maintained strict control over his band of Marvel characters, which means he dabbles in every part of the company. He is involved with Toy Biz products from design to manufacture to marketing; he is working with the publishing division to develop comic books that appeal to younger kids; and he has been instrumental in Marvel's licensing boom. Through licensing, other companies pay Marvel to use its characters in marketing their products. For example, Activision pays Marvel to use Spider-Man in such video games as Mysterio's Menace.

Arad's biggest success came about when he brought his superhero friends to life on television and in the movies. When he joined Marvel in the early 1990s, Arad encountered resistance when he decided to move the company into TV and film. At the time, the comic book market was sluggish and it seemed no one was interested in seeing Marvel characters on any size screen. Arad thought otherwise, and in 1992 he produced the *X-Men* animated series, which appeared on Fox Kids' Network. It was a daring move, since the *X-Men* had a strong fan following, but was not well known by the general public. Arad, however, believed the story had a special appeal for kids, since it focused on the exploits of a group of outsiders (known as mutants because of their special powers) who are shunned by society because they are different.

Arad proved that he had a special knack for knowing what kids like. The series became one of the highest rated television shows on the Fox Network, and Arad went on to produce other Marvel animated series, including *Iron Man, Fantastic Four, Silver Surfer,* and *X-Men: Evolution.*

Swings into movie theaters

In the late 1990s Arad faced a hard sell when he tried to break into the movie business. In the past, Marvel-based movies had been low-budget efforts that were considered to be big jokes. As a result, Hollywood studios were not open to spending millions of dollars on comic book movies that no one wanted to see. Once again Arad proved that

Avi Arad (left) and director Sam Raimi on the set of Spider-Man 2.
R. J. Capak/WireImage.com.

he knew his audience. In 1998 he co-produced *Blade,* the story of an immortal warrior who battles an underworld of vampires bent on destroying the human race. Released by New Line Cinema, the movie earned three times more than it cost to make. Comic book fans praised Arad for remaining true to the Marvel character, and reviewers considered it to be a high-quality action film. As Arad told *Filmforce,* "After that, people were listening very carefully. Very carefully."

In 2000 Arad finally opened the Marvel movie floodgates when he co-produced *X-Men* for the big screen. The movie earned almost $300 million worldwide, and featured respected English actors Sir Ian McKellan (1939–) and Patrick Stewart (1940–), as well as American actress Halle Berry (c. 1968–). It also made a star out of a then-unknown Australian actor named Hugh Jackman (1968–), who played a character named Wolverine.

After that, it seemed Arad could do no wrong. In 2002 *Spider-Man* swung into movie theaters, breaking box office records along the way. It earned over $800 million worldwide and became one of the ten highest grossing films of all time. The success of the first movie spawned a sequel, *Spider-Man 2,* which was released in 2004. Both movies were co-produced with Sony Pictures, and both starred actor Tobey McGuire (1975–) as Peter Parker, alias Spider-Man.

For Arad, bringing the webbed hero to film was more than a business, it was a passion. That passion sparked the release of *The Hulk* and

Daredevil in 2003. And in 2004, along came *The Punisher*, *Spider-Man 2*, *Man-Thing*, and *Blade 3: Trinity*. By mid-2004 there were many other movies already in the pipeline, including *Fantastic Four*, *Ghost Rider*, and *Elektra,* which features the female ninja assassin introduced in *Daredevil,* played by TV actress Jennifer Garner (1972–).

A kid at heart

Some of the Marvel films did better than others. For example, *The Hulk* was not well received either by fans or critics. But Arad believes in every one, and he sees the potential in all of them. In addition, he makes believers out of others. Ang Lee (1954–), who directed *The Hulk,* told Bowles that before he looked at the script he knew very little about the green superhero. The director realized, however, that he had to do a good job because Arad "cares so much about his characters that it causes you to care just as much."

As president and CEO of Marvel Studios, Arad has become a powerful force in the Hollywood community, and because of his influence comic books have re-emerged as a respected form of entertainment. But he is not the typical business tycoon; he is a walking, talking ad for his company. Instead of humdrum suits and ties, Arad wears T-shirts emblazoned with Marvel characters and puts superhero pins on the lapels of his leather jacket. He is also known for sporting a Spider-Man ring on his pinky finger and traveling around on his Harley motorcycle.

It is obvious that Arad is a savvy businessman. The seven Marvel films that he has co-produced since 1998 have grossed more than $2 billion, and in 2003 *Premier* magazine listed him as number forty-four on its annual "Power 100 List." But in the end, Arad is successful because he loves what he does. He may be president of Marvel Studios, but as he told Bowles, while sitting in his office cluttered with action figures and cereal box toys, "I don't think of myself that way. I'm really just a kid inside."

For More Information

Books

Raviv, Dan. *Comic Wars*. New York: Broadway Books, 2002.

Periodicals

Amdur, Meredith. "Marvel Says Super-Size Me." *Daily Variety* (January 20, 2004): pp. 1–2.

Web sites

Bowles, Scott. "Marvel's Chief: A Force Outside, A Kid Inside." *USA Today* (June 5, 2003). http://www.usatoday.com/life/movies/news/2003-06-05-marvel_x.htm (accessed on April 6, 2004).

"A Chat With Marvel's Hollywood Icon: Interview With Avi Arad." *Filmforce: IGN.com* (February 10, 2004). http://filmforce.ign.com/articles/491/491232p1.html (accessed on April 6, 2004).

Last, Jonathan V. "To 'Hellboy' and Back.' *CBSNews.com* (April 2, 2004). http://www.cbsnews.com/stories/2004/04/02/opinion/main610078.shtml (accessed on April 6, 2004).

Marvel Enterprises. http://www.marvel.com (accessed on April 7, 2004).

Spider-Man 2: The Official Web site. http://spiderman.sonypictures.com (accessed on April 6, 2004).

Jean-Bertrand Aristide

July 15, 1953 • Port-Salut, Haiti

Political leader, priest

Jean-Bertrand Aristide, the former president of Haiti, has had a political history as troubled as that of his country. At one time the priest-turned-politician was considered to be the savior of Haiti's poorest citizens. By 2004 many people felt that, despite his good intentions, Aristide had become a corrupt leader who was no longer capable of running his country. Aristide has twice served as president of Haiti. In 1991, less than a year after becoming the country's first democratically elected president, he was overthrown by opposition groups. He was again elected president in 2000, but in February of 2004 he left office amid controversy. U.S. officials claimed that Aristide had resigned; the ousted president has insisted that he was forced to resign. While in exile in the Central African Republic, Aristide stated that he believed he was still the legal and true president of Haiti. He told Amy Goodman on the Znet Web site, "[The people of Haiti] are still fighting in a peaceful way for their elected President. I cannot betray them."

U·X·L newsmakers • volume 1

23

Titide, the political priest

Jean-Bertrand Aristide was born on July 15, 1953, in the fishing village of Port-Salut, Haiti, to parents who were farmers. The occupation of his parents was not uncommon, since the majority of Haitians make a small living by farming. The unique thing was that Joseph and Marie Solanges Aristide, although poor, were educated. According to statistics released by the United Nations (UN) in 2000, fifty percent of the people in Haiti cannot read or write. Joseph died when Jean-Bertrand was only three months old. Marie Solanges then packed up her young son and his older sister and moved to Haiti's capital, Port-au-Prince,

"In order for peace to reign, one must speak the truth."

where her children would have a better chance of receiving an education. An education, she knew, would help them rise out of poverty.

When he was six years old Aristide began studying at a primary school run by the Society of St. Francis de Sales, an order of Roman Catholic priests known as the Salesians. The main mission of the Salesians is to serve the poor. Aristide proved to be an exceptional student. In 1974 he earned a bachelor's degree from the College Notre Dame in Cap-Haitien, Haiti. He then traveled to the Dominican Republic to study for the priesthood at the Salesian Seminary. Aristide then returned to Haiti, where he studied philosophy at the Grand Seminaire Notre Dame and psychology at the State University of Haiti. He also studied in Rome, Israel, and at the University of Montreal in Canada. As a result of his travels, Aristide learned to speak six languages (Spanish, English, Hebrew, Italian, German, and Portuguese), in addition to Creole, the native language of Haiti, and French, the official language of the country. He also studied music and learned to play several instruments, including guitar, piano, and saxophone.

After he became a priest in 1983, Aristide was assigned to a small parish just outside Port-au-Prince called St. Joseph. He was soon transferred to St. Jean Bosco, a larger parish in the heart of the Port-au-Prince

Snapshot: History of Haiti

Haiti is a tiny country located to the south of the United States, in the Caribbean Sea. It occupies the western portion of the island of Hispaniola; the Dominican Republic occupies the eastern portion. Haiti is small, about the size of Maryland, but it is densely populated. About 95 percent of the people who live there are black; they are descendants of the African slaves who worked on the French sugar plantations early in Haiti's history.

In 1492, during his exploration of the Americas, Christopher Columbus discovered the island of Hispaniola and established a Spanish settlement near the present city of Cap-Haitien. By the 1500s, more and more Spanish planters were drawn to the region and slaves from Africa were imported to work the large plantations. In 1697 Spain ceded, or transferred, the western third of the island (now Haiti) to the French. Under French rule, Haiti became one of the wealthiest communities in the Caribbean, and one of the largest producers of sugar and coffee.

By the late 1700s nearly half a million black slaves were living in Haiti. Although they comprised the majority of the population, they were at the bottom of the ethnic hierarchy. The political power was concentrated in the hands of mulattos (people of mixed black and white background) and light-skinned descendants of French landowners. This created a tension between the various groups, which simmered throughout Haiti's history. From 1791 through 1803 the country was rocked by a slave rebellion, led by General Toussaint L'Ouverture (c. 1743–1803), a free slave who had risen in the ranks of the French army. By 1801 General L'Ouverture controlled the entire island. That same year he established a constitution that abolished slavery. In 1804 former slave Jean-Jacques Dessalines (1758–1806) declared Haiti an independent state, free from France's rule. Dessalines called himself emperor and seized all white-owned land.

The remainder of the nineteenth century was marked by frequent and often violent shifts in political power, with twenty-two changes of government between 1843 and 1915. In 1915, because there seemed no end to the constant conflict, the United States stepped in and occupied Haiti until 1934. Following the departure of U.S. troops, the country endured a succession of leaders. One of them was Dumarsais Estime, the first black president of the republic, who took office in 1946. Two subsequent regimes were overthrown, and six held power, before François Duvalier was elected president in 1957. In 1964, Duvalier proclaimed himself president for life. When he died in 1971, he was succeeded by his nineteen-year-old son, Jean-Claude.

slums. Aristide quickly earned a reputation as a champion of the poor. He spent countless hours working at orphanages and youth centers in the poorest and roughest neighborhoods of the capital city. He was also known as a fiery speaker who used the pulpit to spread his political message. Although small in size (he is only five-foot four inches tall), his words were powerful. Aristide, lovingly nicknamed "Titide" (Tiny Aristide) by his followers, spoke out against the military government that had oppressed the Haitian people for most of the twentieth century.

Takes on the Tontons

In particular, Aristide denounced the Duvaliers, a family of Haitians who had been in power since the late 1950s. Until the family was overthrown in 1986, both François "Papa Doc" Duvalier (1907–1971) and his son Jean-Claude "Baby Doc" (1951–), ruled the country through military might. "Papa Doc" created a private army, known as the Tontons Macoutes, whose sole purpose was to rid the country of all opposition. Anyone suspected of opposing the Duvaliers was bullied, kidnapped, or murdered. The army also swept the streets, robbing and killing at random. The people of Haiti lived in constant terror. The majority of them also lived in squalor, since the Duvaliers and their followers, who made up about ten percent of the population, controlled all the wealth.

The Duvaliers, and the military governments that came after them, felt threatened by Aristide. He was a charismatic man, whose kind heart was apparent to the hundreds of people who crowded his church services. He was also being heard across the country, since his sermons were broadcast on the Roman Catholic station, Radio Soleil.

As a result, the number of Aristide's followers was growing by the thousands. In addition, Aristide's sermons were starting to become more radical, as he called for the masses to rise up and claim their rights. Although the tiny priest did not condone violence as a means for change, he did not discourage it, either. As a matter of fact, Aristide was known for quoting a certain passage from the Bible: "And he that hath no sword, let him sell his garment, and buy one" (Luke 22: 36).

The military rulers demanded that the Catholic Church stop Aristide from stirring up the Haitian people. When church leaders were unable to do so, the Tontons stepped in. Several attempts were made on Aristide's life, and on September 11, 1988, his church was attacked while he was saying mass. More than a dozen people were killed, over seventy were seriously wounded, and St. Jean Bosco was burned to the ground. Two weeks later, Aristide was expelled from the Salesian Order and the Vatican (the head of the Roman Catholic Church in Rome) ordered him to transfer out of Haiti.

Following the attacks, Aristide's followers became more loyal than ever. They viewed him as a true holy man, a prophet who would lead them out of their misery. And because he had escaped death over and over, they called him "Mister Miracles." When news got out that Aristide was going to be transferred, tens of thousands of Haitians stormed the streets in what would become the largest demonstration in Haiti's history. They physically blocked access to the airport, forcing Aristide to remain in the country. Aristide stayed and continued to help the poor, even though he had no official church. He helped create a medical center, ran a halfway house for young runaways, and established workshops so that people could become skilled craftsmen.

First presidency: 1991

By the end of the 1980s the military force in Haiti had escalated out of control. World peacekeeping organizations such as the UN and the Organization of American States finally stepped in and demanded that a free election take place. At first Aristide was reluctant to become a presidential candidate. His followers, fearful that the Tontons would take control, begged him to run. On October 18, 1990, Aristide entered the race and called his campaign the *Lavalas* (cleansing flood). A record number of Haitians flocked to the polls, eager to vote in the country's first free election. Aristide won by a landslide, taking almost 68 percent of the popular vote. Aristide supporters danced in the streets, sure that their nightmare was over. Aristide's opposition, composed of the wealthy and the military, viewed him as a threat to their way of life.

Aristide took office on February 7, 1991, determined to focus on social reform. One of his goals was to launch a national literacy program so that even the poorest Haitians could learn how to support themselves. He was also determined to purge the government of corrupt officials from former administrations. Many leaders were asked to retire; some army officers, judges, and police suspected of past violence were jailed. There was an uneasy peace in Haiti, but it did not last long.

It soon became obvious that Aristide, suspicious of the past, could not work with opposition leaders who remained in office. In addition, he formed his own personal army of street gangs who were encouraged to avenge past wrongs. Such eye-for-an-eye justice disturbed many outside of Haiti. The country's military opposition resurfaced, and on September 30, 1991, just seven months into his term, Aristide was overthrown by Raoul Cedras (1950–), a general in the Haitian military.

The Tontons Macoutes was re-formed as the Front for the Advancement and Progress of Haiti, and Cedras launched a new reign of terror. Anyone aligned with Aristide was silenced, which resulted in public executions and widespread torture. Aristide, who had fled to Venezuela and then to the United States, pleaded with world leaders for help. International peacekeeping groups, including the UN and the United States, responded. For almost three years they exerted pressure, both economic and military, to reinstate Aristide. Over and over again their efforts stalled. In September of 1994, more than twenty thousand U.S. troops were sent to Haiti to face the Cedras regime, and a month later Aristide was finally allowed to return to his country and serve out the remainder of his term. According to the constitution of Haiti, a president's term lasts five years.

When Aristide's term ended in February of 1996, he was not allowed to run again, since the constitution of Haiti does not allow for consecutive terms. Aristide was succeeded by Réné Préval, an ally of Aristide and his prime minister since 1991.

Second presidency: 2001

In 1994 Aristide resigned from the priesthood. Not because he had lost his faith, he explained to Patrick Samway in *America,* but "because it gave me the free space in which to work." In 1996 he married Mildred Trouillot, a lawyer who had served as an adviser to Aristide's government. After leaving office and resigning from the priesthood, Aristide continued to fight for the underprivileged, in Haiti as well as around the world. For example, he founded the Aristide Foundation for Democracy, an organization that worked to find solutions to problems facing developing nations.

Aristide also began work on a campaign to become the president of Haiti for a second time. In late 1996 he formed a new political party, the Fanmi Lavalas (FL), or the Lavalas Family Party. The FL swept the Senate elections in May of 2000. Haiti's legislative body, like the U.S. Congress, is divided into two houses: the Senate and the Chamber of Deputies. Parties who opposed Aristide merged to form the Convergence Democratique (CD) and claimed that the elections were fixed. The CD boycotted the November of 2000 presidential elections, and when Aristide walked away with almost 92 percent of the popular vote, they cried foul. Since Aristide had run virtually unopposed, they did not accept him as the true president. When Aristide took over the presidency on February 7, 2001, the CD named Gerard Gourgue as the head of its own government.

The Haiti that Aristide inherited in 2001 was utterly in ruins. The unemployment rate was at an all-time high, roads were impassable, education and health care were in short supply, and drug trafficking was widespread. Once considered the poorest country in the Western Hemisphere, Haiti had become one of the poorest countries in the world. Aristide promised to create jobs and to provide basic necessities, including safe housing and access to clean water. Because of constant conflict with the CD, however, Aristide had little time to make good on his campaign slogan of "Peace in the mind, peace in the belly."

In December of 2001, opposition forces attempted to overthrow Aristide. Aristide supporters responded by setting fire to CD headquarters. The result was a continuing battle between political forces. As a result Haiti continued its downward spiral, and by 2003 the country was in worse shape than ever. In April the UN declared Haiti to be in a state of emergency. According to UN reports, 56 percent of Haitians suffered from malnutrition and only 46 percent had access to clean drinking water.

End of the Aristide era

By the end of 2003 many groups in Haiti, including labor unions and human rights organizations, were calling for Aristide to resign. Even some of his most loyal supporters felt betrayed. In February of 2004 a rebel group calling itself the Revolutionary Artibonite Resistance Front seized Gonaives, Haiti's fourth largest city. The group was led by Guy Philippe, a former police chief. By late February the rebels controlled Haiti's second largest city, Cap-Haitien, which caused Haiti to be split directly in half, with Aristide in control in the south and rebel groups controlling the north.

Aristide's security forces, known as the *chimeres,* battled the rebel army, but they also clashed with any group that opposed the president. They attacked student protesters with machetes, pistols, and rocks, and roamed the streets looting stores, burning cars, and sometimes killing innocent people. Hundreds of Haitians were killed or wounded in the crossfire.

During peace negotiations that ensued, the rebel leaders would accept nothing but Aristide's resignation. Aristide held fast and refused to step down until the end of his term in 2006. By late February, the international community was again poised to intervene. In a February 27, 2004, address reported on the CNN Web site, U.S. Secretary of State Colin Powell (1937–) made a plea: "I know Aristide has the interest of the Haitian people at heart. I hope that he will examine [the decision to resign] carefully considering the interests of the Haitian people."

On February 29, 2004, Aristide reportedly took the plea to heart. In the early hours of the morning he signed documents to officially resign, and then boarded a plane and flew to the Central African Republic. At first the press reported that Aristide had resigned of his own free will, but Aristide began to give interviews that suggested otherwise. According to Steve Miller and Joseph Curl of the *Washington Times,* the president-in-exile accused the United States of kidnapping him. In an interview with the Associated Press and CNN, Aristide declared, "[My captors] were not Haitian forces. They were …

Americans and Haitians together, acting to surround the airport, my house, the palace. Agents were telling me that if I don't leave they would start shooting and killing in a matter of time."

U.S. officials denied the accusations. In the same *Washington Times* article, Secretary of State Powell responded that "Mr. Aristide was not kidnapped. We did not force him on the airplane. He went on the plane willingly.... It was Mr. Aristide's decision to resign." In interview after interview, Aristide insisted that he was forced out of his country. He also insisted that he was not a man of violence, but a man of peace. In a March 8, 2004, interview on the *CNN* Web site, he commented, "Before the elections of the year 2000, which led me for the second time to the National Palace in Haiti, I had talked about peace. And throughout in the National Palace, throughout my tenure, I talked about peace. And today I continue to talk about peace."

Nowhere to go

In 2004, however, Haiti was not a peaceful country. By April, nearly four thousand troops from the United States, Canada, France, and Chile were stationed there trying to keep the peace. It was hoped that elections would result in a new democratic government, but considering the country's history, the outlook was grim. One thing was certain: Aristide would not be returning home. As provisional president Boniface Alexandre commented to Robert Novak of CNN, "He cannot come back to Haiti."

In March of 2004 Aristide received temporary asylum in Jamaica, and in June he and his family took up residence in South Africa. Many in South Africa were not eager to accept him, but government officials agreed to open its doors, seeing the situation as a temporary one. In a press conference on May 31, as quoted on *AllAfrica.com,* South African Deputy Foreign Minister Aziz Pahad welcomed the ousted president, saying, "President Aristide, his family and aides will remain in the country until the situation in Haiti has stabilized to the extent that they can return."

For More Information

Books

"Jean-Bertrand Aristide." *Contemporary Black Biography.* Volume 6. Detroit, MI: Gale Group, 1994.

"Jean-Bertrand Aristide." *Worldmark Encyclopedia of the Nations: World Leaders.* Farmington Hills, MI: Gale Group, 2003.

"Haiti." *Worldmark Encyclopedia of the Nations,* 10th ed., 6 vols. Gale Group, 2001.

Periodicals

Padgett, Tim, and Kathie Klarreich. "One More Show of Force: The U.S. Military Returns to Haiti to Try to Stop the Violence." *Time* (March 15, 2004).

Samway, Patrick H. "Rebuilding Haiti: An Interview with Jean-Bertrand Aristide." *America* (February 15, 1997): p. 12.

Samway, Patrick H. "When Mayhem is the Rule." *Time* (March 8, 2004).

Web Sites

Bowman, Jo. "Aristide Begins Asylum in South Africa." *AllAfrica.com: South Africa.* (June 2, 2004) http://allafrica.com/stories/200406020177.html (accessed on June 9, 2004).

Goodman, Amy. "Goodman Interviews Aristide." *ZNet* (March 8, 2004). http://www.zmag.org/content/showarticle.cfm?SectionID=36&ItemID=5111 (accessed May 4, 2004).

Koinange, Jeff, Lucia Newman, and Barbara Starr. "Aristide Appeals for Peace in Haiti." *CNN* (March 8, 2004). http://www.cnn.com/2004/WORLD/americas/03/08/haiti (accessed on May 5, 2004).

Miller, Steve, and Joseph Curl. "Aristide Accuses U.S. of Forcing His Ouster." *Washington Times* (March 2, 2004). http://www.washtimes.com/national/20040302-124204-5668r.htm (accessed on May 5, 2004).

Newman, Lucia, John King, and John Zarrella. "Powell to Aristide: Do What's Best for Haitian People." *CNN* (February 27, 2004). http://www.cnn.com/2004/WORLD/americas/02/27/haiti.revolt0630/index.html (accessed on May 5, 2004).

Novak, Robert. "Haiti after Aristide." *CNN* (March 25, 2004). http://www.cnn.com/2004/ALLPOLITICS/03/25/haiti (accessed on May 5, 2004).

Jack Black

April 7, 1969 • *Santa Monica, California*

Actor, singer, musician

Jack Black is a one-man dynamo—a manic, scruffy ball of energy who has quietly been shaking up the entertainment world for years. Acting steadily since the mid-1990s, Black usually took on smaller roles that were usually quirky, but always unforgettable. He also became one-half of a comedy rock duo called Tenacious D, which played regularly in small comedy clubs in California. As a result, Black developed a cult following of fans, who watched and waited for him to break out as a star. In 2003 fans got their wish, when Black skidded onto the screen as rocker-turned-teacher Dewey Finn in the blockbuster *School of Rock*. Almost overnight, Jack Black became a household name.

Product of rocket science

Jack Black was born April 7, 1969, in Santa Monica, California, to Tom and Judy Black, both satellite engineers. In a 2003 *Newsweek* interview with Devin Gordon, Black admitted it was ironic that both his parents were rocket scientists. He also put a Jack Black spin on the situation: "They're rocket scientists. I'm a rock scientist."

While Black was growing up his parents fought constantly, which finally led them to divorce when he was ten years old. The separation had a profound effect on Black. In search of attention, he turned to acting. Black appeared in his first television commercial, for Atari, when he was thirteen. "I knew that if my friends saw me on TV, it would be the answer to all my prayers," he told Gordon, "because … everyone would know I was awesome. And I was awesome—for three days. Then it wore off. But it gave me the hunger." Black fol-

> **"There's a little bit of acting in my music, and there's always a little music in my acting, so it's kind of like the peanut butter cups: 'You've got your chocolate in my peanut butter.'"**

lowed his Atari commercial with a Smurfberry Crunch ad, which he admitted wasn't nearly as cool.

After divorcing Judy Black, Tom Black moved out of the country and started a new family. Feeling abandoned, Jack became moody and started to act out. He turned to drugs and began stealing money from his mother. A frustrated Judy sent the boy to an alternative school in Culver City, California, where therapy was part of the curriculum. While there, Black was encouraged by one of his teachers to channel his energy through acting. After getting back on track, Black transferred to a private school called Crossroads in Santa Monica. After graduating in 1987, he enrolled at the University of California at Los Angeles (UCLA).

More than a Belushi clone

In 1989 Black left UCLA to join The Actors' Gang, a Los Angeles-based acting troupe co-founded in 1981 by Tim Robbins (1959–). At

Will Ferrell: Partner in Comedy

It seems that everywhere Jack Black goes, Will Ferrell is not too far behind. In 2003, according to *Entertainment Weekly*'s annual list of top entertainers, Black had the dubious distinction of sharing the title of favorite Hollywood class clown with Ferrell. At the 2004 Academy Awards, the two cracked up viewers when they shared a microphone and sang the "get off the stage" song. And in April of 2004, it was announced that Black and Ferrell were slated to star in an upcoming comedy about two Los Angeles. motorcycle cops. The two have been so closely linked that many people often wonder who is funnier—Black or Ferrell?

Best known for the many characters he created on the long-running television series *Saturday Night Live (SNL),* Will Ferrell was born on July 16, 1968, in Irvine, California. He began his impersonations in high school when he was in charge of broadcasting the daily announcements. Ferrell graduated from the University of Southern California with a degree in sports journalism, and worked briefly as a sports announcer. At the same time, he performed stand-up comedy at local clubs and coffee houses. When he realized he preferred comedy, Ferrell began taking workshops at a local community college. He soon joined The Groundlings, an Los Angeles-based comedy improv group. It was while working with The Groundlings that he was discovered for *Saturday Night Live.*

Ferrell appeared on *Saturday Night Live* from 1995 to 2002, and is known for creating such memorable characters as Craig the Spartan cheerleader, and for his uncanny impersonations of famous persons such as President George W. Bush (1946–). Ferrell's movie career began during his stint on *Saturday Night Live.* His movie titles include *A Night at the Roxbury* (1998), featuring his *SNL* club-hopping character Steve Butabi, *Zoolander* (2001), and *Old School* (2003).

In 2003 Ferrell had his first starring role playing a six-foot-three-inch, yellow-tight-wearing Christmas gnome in the movie *Elf.* Ferrell gave Black a run for his money at the box office when *Elf* proved to be a surprise hit, bringing in $150 million dollars. As a result Ferrell, like Black, seemed to have his pick of roles. He followed *Elf* with the movie *Anchorman* (2004), and signed on to appear in a film by famous director Woody Allen (1935–). He was also chosen to star in the movie *A Confederacy of Dunces,* based on a novel by American author John Kennedy O'Toole (1937–1967). Jack Black had also been considered for the role.

the time, Robbins was best known for his performance as the rookie pitcher in *Bull Durham* (1989), but he was also about to break out as a director. In 1992 Robbins directed his first movie, *Bob Roberts,* and he cast Black in his first film role, as a crazed fan. Their collaboration would continue throughout the 1990s, with Black appearing in two more movies directed by Robbins: *Dead Man Walking* (1995) and *Cradle Will Rock* (1999).

In addition to appearing in Robbins-directed films, Black accumulated a number of other movie credits, usually playing the wacky best friend, as he did in *The Cable Guy* (1996) or *Bongwater* (1998). Black also took bit parts on such television shows as *Life Goes On, Northern Exposure,* and *The X-Files.* He was definitely starting to get noticed, especially by critics, who often compared him to the comedian John Belushi (1949–1982), who first gained fame on the late-night comedy series *Saturday Night Live.*

On the surface, the comparison was easy to see. At five-foot seven inches tall and weighing about two hundred pounds, Black, like Belushi, is short and stocky. He also shares the same wild-eyed look, devilish grin, and animated eyebrows. But it was also clear that Black was not a Belushi clone; he was an actor who brought a unique talent to his many roles. That talent became apparent when he appeared in *High Fidelity* (2000), a movie based on the novel by popular English author Nick Hornby (1957–) and starring John Cusack (1966–). Cusack, a friend of Black's since their Actors' Gang days, suggested Black for the movie.

Although *High Fidelity* starred John Cusack as record store owner Rob Gordon, the main draw of the movie was Jack Black, who played Barry, the obnoxious record store clerk with an almost encyclopedic knowledge of all things vinyl. Barry does little actual work. Instead, he and a fellow clerk spend most of their time making fun of customers and quizzing each other on music trivia. The record store scenes highlight Black's whip-smart acting abilities, but the real treat takes place at the end of the film. Barry, who has hinted about his singing aspirations throughout the movie, takes the stage and steals the show by belting out a classic tune by American R&B singer Marvin Gaye (1939–1984).

Half of a tenacious duo

For those who have followed Black's career, it was not surprising that he took so easily to the microphone in *High Fidelity.* Since 1994, in addition to being an actor, Black has also been part of a rock band known as Tenacious D. Black formed the two-man group with Kyle Gass, whom he met while performing with The Actors' Gang. In a *People* interview with Jason Lynch, Black confided that at first he and Gass were "archenemies," but that eventually they worked out their differences and soon were spending a lot of time in Gass's apartment, writing songs, playing music, and dreaming about forming a band. They named their group Tenacious D, which stands for "tenacious defense," a term regularly used by sports announcer Marv Albert (1944–).

The D (as the group is referred to by its fans) started out as a regular band, but Black and Gass quickly realized that their strength was in parody. This means that they poke fun at anything that comes their way, including heavy metal rockers who take themselves too seriously and the music industry in general. Essentially they are heavy metal comedians: two middle-aged, overweight men who tear up the stage like veteran rock stars. According to Cusack, who spoke with reporter Michael Salkind of the *Colorado Springs Gazette* in 2000, Tenacious D is "one of the six or seven wonders of the world."

The band drew such a following at local Los Angeles area clubs that the rock duo was soon featured in short spots on the Home Box Office (HBO) show, *Mr. Show with Bob and David.* This led to an appearance in the 1995 movie *Bio-Dome* and a half-hour series in 1999 on HBO called *Tenacious D: The Greatest Band on Earth.*

Black and White

Following his talented turn in *High Fidelity,* Black got his first taste as a leading man while playing opposite Oscar-winning actress Gwyneth Paltrow (1973–) in the comedy *Shallow Hal* (2001). The movie's premise is that Black's character, the superficial Hal Larson, pursues only gorgeous women. During a chance meeting with self-help guru Tony Robbins, Larson is hypnotized so that he is able to see a woman's inner beauty. As a result, he stuns his friends by falling for a 300-pound woman. Critics generally panned the weak comedy, and most felt that Black was miscast as the cynical Larson. On the other hand, it was a turning point in his career, since it was evident that Black felt comfortable as a leading man. Roger Ebert, film critic for the *Chicago Sun-Times,* commented that "in his first big-time starring role, [Black] struts through with the blissful confidence of a man who knows he was born for stardom."

In 2002 Black briefly slipped back into co-star status when he appeared as Lance, the deadbeat brother, in the offbeat comedy *Orange County.* Again, the movie received lackluster reviews, but critics, including Ebert, were wowed by Black's performance. The film was also important for Black because he formed a partnership with the movie's writer that would change his career.

Orange County was written by Mike White (1970–), a pal of Black's who lived next door to him in Hollywood from 1997 to 2000. White, too, was on the verge of making it big. He had written for the popular television shows *Freaks and Geeks* and *Dawson's Creek,* and he had penned the movies *Chuck and Buck* (2000) and *The Good Girl* (2002). Black admitted to Steven Daly of *Entertainment Weekly* that he was "obsessed" with White's quirky style of writing, so he approached his friend about writing a movie specifically for him. He was tired of being offered frat boy Belushi-type roles and wanted something that would showcase his talents. White was up for the challenge, and spent five months designing a custom-made role for Black and crafting a script. The character he developed was Dewey Finn; the movie was *School of Rock* (2003).

School Daze

In *School of Rock,* Black plays Dewey Finn, a down-on-his-luck guitarist and singer who scams his way into becoming a substitute teacher at a posh New York prep school. The scruffy musician has his own unique way of teaching. For homework, he hands out CDs so that his students can study the history of rock, and their daily lessons focus on creating what he calls "musical fusion." Ultimately Finn and his fifth graders form their own group, the School of Rock, and they compete in a citywide battle of the bands. But of course the point is not about winning the contest. As Freddy, the band's ten-year-old drummer explained, "We're on a mission. One great rock show can change the world."

The character of Dewey Finn is everything about Black all rolled into one: he has Black's abundant energy, his love of rock and roll, his musical talent, and his frantic personality. As Black explained to Edna Gundersen in *USA Today,* he "scientifically figured [Dewey Finn] is 92% me. There's 8% that's not me." In the same article, however, film writer White was quick to point out that Finn is not a Xerox copy of Black. "Jack is a conscientious professional who takes his job seriously, and he isn't bouncing off the walls 24/7."

School of Rock brought in more than $20 million at the box office when it opened in October of 2003. The movie drew praise for writer White, who also costarred as Finn's uptight roommate, Ned Schneebly. Director Richard Linklater (1961–) also earned kudos for the project. Linklater, who directed 1993's *Dazed and Confused,* is a dedicated rock buff; he painstakingly made sure that all music references in the movie were accurate. In addition, it was Linklater's idea to cast children who were musicians as Dewey Finn's students. All the kids in the movie sing and play their own instruments.

Jack Black poses with his young co-stars at the Hollywood premiere of School of Rock. *AP/Wide World Photos. Reproduced by permission.*

Goblets of praise

Without a doubt, however, *School of Rock* was Jack Black's movie. It established him as a certified star, and critics, to quote Dan Snierson in *Entertainment Weekly,* raised "goblets of gush" in his honor. Black even received a Golden Globe nomination as best leading actor in a musical or comedy. Golden Globes are awarded each year by members of the Hollywood Foreign Press for outstanding achievement in film and television.

Following the movie's release, Black went on a nonstop whirl of interviews, appearing on every program from *Good Morning America* to the *Tonight Show*. In interviews he gave a glimpse into his personal life, making it clear that he is not the party animal that people perceive him to be. In fact, White explained to Gordon that in all the years he lived next door to his portly pal, they never had a single party. Instead, Black spends as much time as he can with his longtime girlfriend, actress and writer Laura Kightlinger. He is a self-proclaimed hermit, whose favorite pastimes include sleeping late, all-night movie marathons, and playing video games on his Xbox.

Given his white-hot status, however, there is not much time for Black to relax. In 2004 he appeared in *Envy* with Ben Stiller (1966–), and then lent his voice to the animated film *Shark Tale*. He was also tapped by English director Peter Jackson (1961–) to star in a remake of *King Kong*. Black especially hoped his newfound clout would spark interest in his own pet project, a script called *Tenacious D in the Pick of Destiny*. When asked by Daly what might be next on his plate, Black replied as only he can, "I'll probably have to do something stretchy. After the D-movie, of course. But then? Stretcha-letcha ding-dong."

For More Information

Periodicals

Daly, Steve. "Jack Black Slept Here." *Entertainment Weekly* (October 17, 2003): pp. 26–30.

Gordon, Devin. "Jumpin' Jack Black: He's a Gas, Gas, Gas." *Newsweek* (September 29, 2003): p. 52.

Hay, Carla. "Black Back from Media Blitz." *Billboard* (October 25, 2003): p. 18.

Lynch, Jason. "Dude Awakening: In School of Rock He Rules, but Jack Black Could Use Some Peace and Quiet." *People Weekly* (October 13, 2003): p. 75.

Salkind, Michael. "Tenacious D Parodies Really Rock." *Colorado Springs Gazette* (April 24, 2000): p. 10.

Snierson, Dan. "Jack Black and Will Ferrell: Class Clowns." *Entertainment Weekly* (December 26, 2003): p. 40.

Web Sites

Ebert, Roger. "*Shallow Hal.*" *Chicago Sun-Times* (November 9, 2001). http://www.suntimes.com/ebert/ebert_reviews/2001/11/110903.html (accessed on April 19, 2004).

Grosz, Christy. "Dialogue: Jack Black." *Hollywood Reporter* (March 24, 2004). http://www.hollywoodreporter.com/thr/crafts/feature_display.jsp?vnu_content_id=1000473949 (accessed on April 21, 2004).

Gundersen, Edna. "The Lighter Side of Jack Black." *USA Today* (September 28, 2003). http://www.usatoday.com/life/movies/news/2003-09-28-black_x.htm (accessed on April 21, 2003).

Orlando Bloom

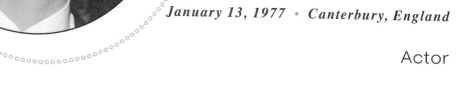

January 13, 1977 • Canterbury, England

Actor

Orlando Bloom is best known for playing the elf warrior Legolas Greenleaf in the epic film trilogy *The Lord of the Rings*. His ability as an actor was appreciated by critics, but the bigger story was that over the course of the three films Bloom attracted an enormous number of fans. Although his naturally dark features were disguised by a waist-length blonde wig, blue contact lenses, and pointy ears, young girls the world over discovered a new heartthrob. Bloom's success as Legolas opened doors for the classically trained English actor, who has gone on to appear in a number of other critically acclaimed movies. In addition, he became one of the hottest young properties in Hollywood, making *Entertainment Weekly*'s "It list" in 2003.

Early bloomer

Orlando Bloom was born on January 13, 1977, in Canterbury, England. His mother, Sonia, ran a foreign language school; his father,

Harry, was a human rights activist, lawyer, and author. Before moving to Canterbury the elder Blooms lived in South Africa, where Harry Bloom (1913–1981) was a fierce fighter in the struggle against apartheid, a policy of racial segregation. When Orlando was only four years old, his father died after suffering a stroke. He and his older sister, Samantha, were raised by their mother, who had a profound effect on her children.

Sonia Bloom was a businesswoman, but she was also a true lover of the arts. She even named her son after her favorite English composer, Orlando Gibbons (1583–1625). While growing up, Sonia frequently took Orlando and Samantha to the theater, and encouraged

> **"I'd really like to take a role that doesn't involve a sword."**

both of them to attend drama classes and Bible reading classes. By the age of eight Bloom was appearing in school plays, and he and his sister were competing in local festivals. As Bloom recounted to Siobhan Synnot on the *scotsman.com* Web site, "You had to read out stories or poetry, and we always won."

His introduction to the theater made Bloom decide at an early age that he wanted to be an actor. Acting was also a positive outlet for Bloom, since it helped him work through some early childhood problems. For one thing, as he told Synnot, he was "quite a chubby kid." Part of the chubbiness came about during his recovery from a skiing injury that happened when he was nine—while Bloom was recovering, he moped about the house and ate candy bars. A more serious issue arose when he was diagnosed with severe dyslexia, which means that he has trouble reading and processing language. While attending St. Edmund's School in Canterbury, he was often teased about his poor spelling.

At age thirteen Bloom received another blow when he learned from his mother that Harry Bloom was not his real father. His biological father (and Samantha's as well) was a man named Colin Stone, a

Fast Facts for Orlando Fans

- Bloom considers himself to be incredibly accident prone. He has broken both his legs (in skiing accidents), his nose (a rugby injury), a wrist (while snowboarding), and a toe (crushed by a horse). He has even suffered a few skull fractures. For example, when Bloom was a toddler, he toppled off a kitchen stool.

- While filming *The Lord of the Rings* films in New Zealand, Bloom and the other nine actors who made up the "fellowship of the ring" became so close-knit that they decided to get tattoos. Bloom has the elf symbol for the number nine tattooed on his forearm.

- Bloom is an excellent sculptor. He studied sculpting in school and hopes to one day have his own sculpting studio. As Bloom explained to Catriona Hawatson of the *Sunday Times (UK)*, "It is important to exercise different creative areas of your brain. It balances you."

- Around his neck Bloom wears a number of charms and trinkets. Some of them are gifts, such as a key ring that was given to him by Johnny Depp; others are things that Bloom has found on his travels, such as a shell from Thailand, a prayer baton from India, and a silver ball from Tokyo, Japan.

longtime family friend who was also Bloom's legal guardian. In interviews, Bloom has sometimes seemed uncomfortable talking about the issue, but the revelation does not seem to have caused a great deal of disruption. As he explained to Synnot, "I was lucky, I had two dads.… As long as I can remember, Colin has been a good friend, but I always thought Harry was my real father."

Budding actor

Bloom left St. Edmunds when he was sixteen years old to join the National Youth Theatre in London. After two seasons he won a scholarship to train with the British American Drama Academy. While there he auditioned for parts on television and in theater. Bloom then spent three years studying at the Guildhall School of Music and Drama, a prestigious London school that was the training ground for such newly famous English actors as Ewan McGregor (c. 1971–), Joseph Fiennes (1970–), and Ben Chaplin (c. 1969–). In 1998 Bloom made his first film appearance, a small, one-line part in the movie *Wilde,* about English playwright Oscar Wilde (1854–1900). Several movie offers followed, but a serious accident put a brief crimp in Bloom's career and had a life-changing effect on the budding actor.

When he was twenty-one years old, while shimmying along the drainpipe of a friend's apartment in an attempt to open a window, Bloom fell three stories and broke his back. The possibility that he would be paralyzed was very real. Metal plates were bolted to his spine and he wore a back brace for almost a year. Bloom also endured months of rehabilitation. As he told Allison Glock of *Gentleman's Quarterly,* the accident made him realize how lucky he was to be alive. He recounted to Glock how one person in particular helped him to put things in perspective: "I had this one great teacher who came to visit and said to me, 'This is going to be the making of you.' And it was."

Miraculously, Bloom recovered enough to return to his regular life at Guildhall. Just two days before graduation, in 1999, he found out from his agent that director Peter Jackson (1961–) had chosen him to appear in his film trilogy *The Lord of the Rings,* which was based on the fantasy trilogy written by English author J.R.R. Tolkien (1892–1973). Originally Bloom had hoped for the role of the human named Faramir, who is introduced in *The Two Towers,* the second film in the series. Jackson, however, felt Bloom was perfect for the role of Legolas Greenleaf, the elf warrior of Mirkwood. Since Legolas is one of the main characters in the story, it meant that Bloom would appear in all three films of the trilogy.

Joins the fellowship

The Lord of the Rings is the epic tale of nine warriors (four hobbits, two humans, a dwarf, an elf, and a wizard) who must form a fellowship in order to save their mythical world of Middle Earth from destruction. It is a sweeping adventure story, and bringing it to the screen was a major undertaking. In an interview with Henry Cabot Beck in *Interview* magazine, Bloom admitted that it was more than a little intimidating for his first big role to be in such a major movie. The young actor spent months preparing to play Legolas, since the role required him to be an expert at archery, sword fighting, and horseback riding. After recovering from his back injury, Bloom welcomed the physical challenge. "It was like winning the lottery," he told Beck. "I mean, imagine being flown to this amazing country and being taught how to shoot a bow and arrow, learn to ride horses, and study swordplay."

The "amazing country" was New Zealand, where cast and crew spent almost two years filming the three movies. While in New Zealand, Bloom and his costars became very close, forming almost a family bond. Bloom was considered the daredevil of the bunch, since he spent what free time he had bungee jumping, snowboarding, and learning how to surf. In addition, he performed most of his own stunts. During one scene Bloom fell from his horse and broke a rib. He was back in the saddle within a few days.

The trilogy was released over a three-year period. *The Fellowship of the Ring* was unveiled in 2001, followed by *The Two Towers* in 2002, and *The Return of the King* in 2003. All three movies broke box office records and all three were critically acclaimed. In 2002 Bloom received an award for Best Debut at the Empire Awards, sponsored by the British film magazine *Empire*. He also won the Breakthrough Male honor at the 2002 MTV Movie Awards. At the same time, fans around the world catapulted the young actor to fame. Synnot estimated that after *Fellowship* was released, almost thirty thousand Internet sites sprang up that were devoted to the handsome Brit. Before *The Two Towers* had even opened in theaters, there were over one million Orlando Bloom Web sites. The modest Bloom explained away the phenomenon to Kate Stroup of *Newsweek:* "Legolas is a good, safe guy for girls to pin their dreams on."

Life after Middle Earth

While working on *The Fellowship of the Ring,* Bloom took a small role in director Ridley Scott's *Black Hawk Down* (2001), a movie about the 1993 Battle of Mogadishu in Somalia, East Africa. The film was a case of art imitating life: Bloom played a U.S. Army Ranger who breaks his back falling from a helicopter. The part was small but pivotal, and Bloom was applauded for his efforts. Just two years out of school, the twenty-three-year-old actor had appeared in two of the top movies of 2001, and he was just getting started.

Bloom continued to appear in films that challenge him physically, and he also shared the screen with some of Hollywood's more established heartthrobs. In 2003 he costarred in *Ned Kelly,* a shoot-'em-up movie about a notorious Australian outlaw. Australian hunk Heath Ledger (1979–) played the lead, while Bloom portrayed Joe

Orlando Bloom (left) and Diane Kruger in a movie still from Troy *(2004).* © Warner Brothers Pictures/Zuma/Corbis.

Byrne, a member of Kelly's gang. Although he was in a supporting role, Bloom stole the spotlight. According to Lisa Schwarzbaum in *Entertainment Weekly,* "The effortlessly charismatic Bloom … dims our interest in Ledger every time the two share a scene."

In 2003 Bloom also costarred in a big-budget Disney picture, *Pirates of the Caribbean: The Curse of the Black Pearl,* based on the Disney theme park ride of the same name. This time the leading man was Johnny Depp (c. 1963–), who played Captain Jack Sparrow. Bloom took the role of blacksmith-turned-pirate Will Turner. Once again the fearless actor had to test his skill with a sword. The difference this time was that Will Turner had an onscreen romance, which meant that fans were given a look at Bloom's first onscreen kiss.

More sword and dagger work came his way in 2004, when Bloom joined Brad Pitt (1963–) in the film *Troy*. The movie is an epic account of the Trojan War, the ten-year battle of Greek legend between the Greeks and Trojans. Bloom played Paris, Prince of Troy, who ignites the seeds of war when he carries off the beautiful Helen, queen of Sparta.

Bona fide star

Midway through the making of *Troy, Pirates of the Caribbean* was released, and it became apparent that Bloom's star was ascending in the leading man department. According to *Troy* costar Diane Kruger (who played Helen), when the filming started no one really knew who Bloom was. But when *Pirates* came out, she told the Web site *Teen Hollywood.com* that "it was pretty extraordinary to witness someone going from basically nothing to having girls screaming whenever we stepped out the door."

Bloom seemed to handle his newfound celebrity well, perhaps because he got a few pointers from some of the biggest names in the film business, namely Johnny Depp and Brad Pitt. For example, while shooting *Troy* in Malta, an island nation in the Mediterranean, Bloom and Pitt were mobbed by fans. Bloom explained to Synnot that Pitt was very calm, and directed him to just keep walking: "Don't stop walking and we'll be fine. If you stop, it can get really scary."

But Bloom wanted to be more than just a pinup star; he wanted to sink his teeth into deeper roles. And he managed to do just that by choosing a different kind of part in *The Calcium Kid,* a low budget British comedy released in May of 2004. In sharp contrast to his tan, tousled look as Paris in *Troy,* Bloom transformed himself into a nervous milkman who, through a series of strange coincidences, ends up fighting the world boxing champion. As he told Synnot, "It was just something completely different. I needed to do it."

Bloom also spent 2004 wrapping up work on at least two other films, *Haven,* a crime drama featuring Bill Paxton (1955–), and *Kingdom of Heaven,* which reunited the young actor with *Black Hawk Down* director Ridley Scott. He was also slated to appear in a sequel to *Pirates of the Caribbean.*

From almost dying in a fall in 1998 to starring in some of the biggest movies of the 2000s, Orlando Bloom has experienced an almost meteoric rise to stardom. He has become an international idol for scores of young female fans, and may even become the model for a new generation of stars. Those who know him have described him as charismatic but also sensitive, thoughtful, and polite. Gregor Jordan (c. 1967–), who directed Bloom in *Ned Kelly,* summed it all up when talking to Synnot, stating that Bloom "is going to be huge because he's a good actor and he has incredible presence. There's a reason why girls go crazy for him. There's just something about him that makes people want to sit in the dark and watch him on the movie screen."

For More Information

Periodicals

Beck, Henry Cabot. "Orlando Bloom: Two Roles Under One Belt and Injuries to Rival Jackie Chan." *Interview* (November 2001): pp. 50–52.

Glock, Allison. "Orlando's Magic." *Gentleman's Quarterly* (January 2004).

"Greater Orlando." *People* (January 12, 2004): p. 26.

Schwarzbaum, Lisa. "Ned Kelly: Outback Outlaws Outwit, Outplay, and Outlast the Odds." *Entertainment Weekly* (April 2, 2003): p. 45.

Stroup, Kate. "Orlando Bloom: The Budding of a Heartthrob." *Newsweek* (July 14, 2003): p. 56.

Web Sites

Howatson, Catriona. "What to Look Forward To." *Sunday Times (UK)* (December 30, 2001). http://www.geocities.com/bloomin_fan/UK_Sunday_times.html (accessed on April 23, 2004).

"It List 2003: It Elf, Orlando Bloom." *Entertainment Weekly* (June 27, 2003). http://www.ew.com/ew/article/commentary/0,6115,459112_1_0_,00.html (accessed on April 23, 2004).

"Kruger Stunned by Suddenness of Orlando's Fame." *Teen Hollywood.com* (April 8, 2004). http://www.teenhollywood.com/d.asp?r=65110&cat=1027 (accessed on April 23, 2004).

The Lord of the Rings. http://www.lordoftherings.net/film/trilogy/thefellowship.html (accessed on April 22, 2004).

Synnot, Siobhan. "In Full Bloom." *scotsman.com* (April 18, 2004). http://news.scotsman.com/features.cfm?id=426322004 (accessed on April 22, 2004).

Troy. http://troymovie.warnerbros.com (accessed on April 23, 2004).

Wes Boyd and Eli Pariser

Wes Boyd
c. 1961

Political activist

Eli Pariser
c. 1981 • Camden, Maine

Political activist

In the early 1990s Wes Boyd was flying high as a successful entrepreneur in the computer industry. He earned millions of dollars and made his way into the homes of thousands of PC users, all because of a popular screen saver that featured tiny winged toasters. But by the late 1990s Boyd had left his business behind, and was instead harnessing the power of the Internet as a means for political action. In 1998 he and his wife, Joan Blades, started MoveOn.org as a small-scale response to the impending impeachment of President Bill Clinton. Little did they know that they were starting an online political revolution. By the mid-2000s, after joining forces with a young activist named Eli Pariser, MoveOn supporters numbered in the millions and the organization itself had become what John Heilemann of *Business 2.0* called "one of the country's most influential interest groups, both online and off."

The accidental activists

When Wes Boyd was growing up, he did not plan on changing the world, but he did envision himself working with computers. He was born in the early 1960s, and by the time he was fourteen years old he was hooked on computers and was considered something of a computer prodigy. Boyd attended college for a bit, but dropped out to pursue his passion—software design. For several years he worked as a programmer at the University of California at Berkeley. He then went on to design software for personal computer (PC) users who were blind or visually impaired. In 1987 he made the leap to entertainment

"Our goal is to make it impossible to ignore the anti-war sentiment in this country."

Eli Pariser, *AlterNet*, February 11, 2003.

software design when he formed his own company, Berkeley Systems, along with his wife, Joan Blades.

Boyd was the technical expert and served as the company's chief executive officer (CEO). Blades, who had previously worked as a professional mediator, took on the role of vice president of marketing. A mediator is someone who acts as a negotiator between two parties who are in dispute. Over the years Berkeley Systems grew into a leader in the entertainment software industry, producing such well-known online computer games as "You Don't Know Jack," a game show that challenged a player's knowledge of popular culture. Berkeley Systems' biggest claim to fame, however, was their line of screen savers, which are images that display on the screen when a computer is on but not in use. The company's most popular screen saver consisted of colorful winged toasters. Their business was so lucrative that by the late 1990s Boyd and Blades employed 150 people and were making yearly sales of approximately $30 million.

In 1997 the couple sold Berkeley Systems for a reported $13.8 million, and settled down to enjoy a quiet, peaceful life in their com-

The Ultimate Bake Sale

MoveOn.org uses the Internet to rouse its many members to action in a variety of ways. One of Eli Pariser's ideas was really a very simple one: have a giant bake sale. In April of 2004 Pariser put out a call on MoveOn.org's Web site, asking members across the country to host bake sales, the proceeds of which would go toward financing Senator John Kerry's bid for the presidency. Members responded in droves to the "Bake Back the White House" campaign, and on April 17 more than one thousand bake sales were held from Hawaii to Maine.

Over fourteen thousand creative bakers served up such treats as Beat Bush Brownies and Kerry Karamels, and by day's end, the cross-country bake sale had brought in approximately $750,000. Volunteers also passed out more than forty thousand Kerry flyers and worked to register voters. In an Associated Press story reported on cnews.com, Adam Ruben, a field director of the MoveOn PAC, explained: "We wanted to do a fund-raiser, but we wanted to do it fresher and with a twist. This is a great way to engage a lot of people who have signed a petition online but haven't done anything in their neighborhood."

fortable home located in the Berkeley, California, foothills. That peace was short-lived. In 1998 the United States was rocked by scandal when President Bill Clinton (1946–) was accused of misconduct surrounding an affair he had with White House intern Monica Lewinsky. The investigation and hearings dragged on for months and the president faced impeachment. In the United States, the House of Representatives has the power to bring formal charges (the power of impeachment) against a president that may lead to his removal from office; the Senate hears the case and makes the ultimate decision. Boyd and Blades, like many people, felt that the hearings had gone on for too long, that the president did not deserve to be impeached, and that politicians should get back to the real business of running the country.

In September of 1998 the couple decided to do something. They launched a Web site called MoveOn.org, which included a simple, one-line petition that read: "Congress must immediately censure President Clinton and Move On to pressing issues facing the country." They were essentially calling for a reprimand, not removal from office. Boyd and Blades then e-mailed the petition to one hundred of their friends, and invited them to add their names. "It was supposed to be a flash campaign," Boyd explained in *Time*. "We're in, we're out, we're fixed." The two ex-computer executives, however, were just getting started. Within a week, one hundred thousand people had signed the petition, and just a few months later, more than a half-million people had added their names. The response was so great that Boyd and Blades recruited volunteers via the Web, asking them to hand-deliver petitions to members of the House or to make calls to district offices.

On-line campaigning

President Clinton was impeached by members of the House of Representatives in a vote that went directly along party lines, meaning that the majority of Republican representatives voted for impeachment, while most Democrats voted against it. Clinton was found not guilty by the Senate in January of 1999, but the issue was not over for the members of MoveOn. In June of 1999 the organization established its own political action committee (PAC), a group that raises funds for political candidates who they feel will support its interests. In this case, the MoveOn PAC specifically worked against Republican candidates who had voted for impeachment. Donors were able to contribute online, and within five days of its launch, the MoveOn PAC brought in an astonishing $250,000.

By election day of 2000, the PAC had raised $2 million to help elect four new senators and five new congressional members—all Democrats. This was not the first time that an organization had used the Web to raise funds for candidates, and the amount raised, given the astronomical costs of campaigning, was not very large. But MoveOn had demonstrated that it was successful at reaching the small donor, considering that the average contribution they received was $35. "That may not seem like a lot of money to most people," Blades commented to Terrence McNally of *AlterNet,* "but it was a revolution in fundraising for campaigns from average citizens." MoveOn also proved that fundraising could be relatively inexpensive. Traditional fundraising is primarily done through direct mailings. In this case, there were no printing or postage costs; the biggest expense came from credit card transaction fees.

In less than two years MoveOn had evolved from an online petition site to an organization that influenced elections. It also began to branch out to focus on other issues, including gun control, environmental protection, and campaign finance reform. Although Boyd and Blades maintained control of the site, they did not control the issues.

That was left up to the MoveOn members, who voiced their opinions through ActionForum.com, the site's Internet discussion forum. On the forum, visitors to the site comment on various subjects and offer suggestions for strategy, while other members rank the comments. The comments that receive the highest rankings move to the top and represent the opinions of the majority. MoveOn's priorities are based on this feedback. As Boyd explained to Heilemann, "We do deep listening to our base; we know where they are and what they want to do. We live and breathe response rates."

Pariser, the virtual peacenik

ActionForum became a hotbed of discussion, particulary following the terrorist attacks of September 11, 2001. Based on member feedback, MoveOn launched an online campaign calling for "justice, not escalating violence." Thousands of supporters responded. Boyd and Blades also noticed that other sites were popping up on the Web that shared their viewpoint, but one in particular, called 9-11Peace.org, caught their eye. It had been launched by a twenty-year-old young man named Eli Pariser.

Pariser was born in Camden, Maine, the son of two 1960s peace activists who went on to establish an alternative high school in their small harbor hometown. The Parisers introduced Eli to politics when he was very young, encouraging him to watch or listen to the news and explaining even the most difficult concepts to him. As he told Heather Salerno of the Westchester, N.Y., *Journal News,* "When I heard something on the radio about … nuclear war, I asked and they gave me a straight answer." At age nineteen, Pariser graduated from Simon's Rock College, a progressive school located in Great Barrington, Massachusetts. He briefly considered a career in law after being accepted by the University of Chicago, but instead decided to go to work designing Web pages. His career as a Web designer was cut short by the events of September 11.

Like Boyd and Blades a decade earlier, Pariser wanted to make his voice known. He created an online petition at his Web site that advocated a peaceful response to the terrorist attacks and urged President George W. Bush (1946–) and members of Congress to use "moderation and restraint." Pariser initially e-mailed the link to his site to thirty of his friends; his friends forwarded the link to their friends, and within two weeks more than five hundred thousand people from around the world had added their names to the petition. The site caused such a global buzz that Pariser began receiving calls from news organizations that wanted to know more about the lanky young man. Pariser also received a call from Wes Boyd, who offered advice and financial support. As Pariser told Salerno, "Eli was in the same place as we were when we got started. We got in touch and said, 'Can we help?'"

Boyd did more than help. Not long after, he invited Pariser to merge Web sites and he hired the young activist to become MoveOn's director of international campaigns. Since then, Pariser has become the public face of the organization, appearing at rallies and providing interviews to the press, while Boyd is the organization's president and Web mastermind. According to John Heilemann, MoveOn's co-founder is much more comfortable behind the scenes, offering his technical expertise and tending to the business side of things. As Boyd told Heilemann, MoveOn is a "service business providing connection to the political process, using technology as a lever." Joan Blades serves on the board of directors of MoveOn and is a full-time volunteer.

The power of advertising

Since Pariser joined the organization, MoveOn's membership has nearly tripled. According to 2004 figures, approximately 2.25 million people from around the world are registered members. Pariser spent long hours, sometimes up to eighteen hours a day, making sure that these members were heard and that their concerns were turned into action. He continued to make use of online petitions, letter-writing campaigns, and political fund-raising ($3.5 million was raised for the 2002 congressional elections), and also launched dynamic new initiatives, several of which involved face-to-face activism and grassroots organizing—meaning organizing at the local level. In particular, Pariser and members of MoveOn rallied extensively around a single issue: to prevent an invasion of Iraq by U.S. troops. In the wake of September 11, the U.S. government had purportedly linked the terrorist attacks of September 11 to Saddam Hussein (1937–), the leader of Iraq.

MoveOn became so powerful that it was eventually able to break into traditional areas of advertising, including print, radio, and television. Such advertising is traditionally off-limits to smaller non-profit groups because the cost of advertising is incredibly expensive. In December of 2002 Pariser asked MoveOn members to donate $40,000 to pay for a full-page ad in the *New York Times* that would feature an anti-war appeal. Within a few days, the contributions totaled nearly $400,000. With the extra money, the organization was able to pay for additional anti-war spots on radio and television that appeared in thirteen cities across the United States. The thirty-second televised spot was particularly controversial, and some channels, including CNN, Fox, and NBC refused to air it. Called the Daisy ad, it was a remake of a famous ad that appeared during the 1964 presidential race between Lyndon Johnson (1908–1973) and Barry Goldwater (1909–1998). Both ads feature a young girl plucking petals from a daisy while the threat of nuclear war looms in the distance.

Despite MoveOn's efforts, the United States invaded Iraq in March of 2003, and MoveOn turned its attention toward the 2004 elections and the removal of George W. Bush from office. The organization threw its support behind John Kerry (1943–), the Democratic candidate for president, and took the art of ad campaigning one step closer to the average citizen by creating a unique contest called "Bush in 30 Seconds." The contest invited people to submit homemade thirty-second commercials critiquing a Bush administration policy. More than 1,500 people entered the contest, which was judged online by thousands of MoveOn members. The ultimate winner was chosen by a panel of celebrities, including documentary filmmaker Michael Moore (1954–).

The winning commercial, called "Child's Play," received wide exposure on the Internet, and was broadcast on several television networks. CBS, however, refused to air it during the 2004 Super Bowl, claiming it was too controversial. In mid-2004, MoveOn went to the experts to launch a flurry of anti-Bush ads that were televised and run in theaters as movie trailers. Such Hollywood heavyweights as film director Rob Reiner (1947–), writer Aaron Sorkin (1961–), and musician Moby (1965–), were only too happy to oblige. As Reiner commented to Ronald Brownstein of the *Los Angeles Times,* "We're all on [MoveOn's] e-mail list and we know how effective they are. When they ask us to play a role in getting rid of President Bush, you jump to the task."

Word of mouse

MoveOn had not gone Hollywood, however. Before any of the commercials were broadcast, MoveOn members were asked for their approval. And according to commentators, such tactics have contributed to the organization's amazing success. Despite how large their membership base had become, Boyd and Pariser remained tied to the group's original goal: to provide a voice for ordinary citizens. Their success was also attributed to the no-frills simplicity of their organization. MoveOn has only a handful of staff members, and there are no offices. Employees work out of their homes and connect through e-mail and occasional telephone conferences. Pariser operates out of New York City, from a closet-sized room in an apartment he shares with four roommates and two cats.

By the mid-2000s, MoveOn had grown from a simple idea to become one of the most powerful political forces in the United States. Politicians were sitting up and taking notice, and the rest of the world had realized that Boyd and Pariser were pioneers in a new frontier of online politicking. Hundreds of thousands of dollars could be raised in mere hours and, more important, millions of voices had a quick and easy outlet for action. For Boyd and Pariser, this was the future of politics, and it was all accomplished through word of mouse.

For More Information

Periodicals

Taylor, Chris, and Karen Tumulty. "MoveOn's Big Moment: How an Activist Website with Just Seven Staff Members and No Office is Changing Internet Politics." *Time* (November 24, 2003).

Web Sites

"Anti-Bush Group Organizes Bake Sales across the U.S.A. to Raise Money." *cnews.com* (April 17, 2004). http://cnews.canoe.ca/CNEWS/ WeirdNews/2004/04/17/426758-ap.html (accessed on July 22, 2004).

Brownstein, Ronald. "Tapping Talent, Not Just Names." *Los Angeles Times* (July 4, 2004). http://www.latimes.com/news/politics/la-na-moveon4 jul04,1,6080074.story?coll=la-home-headlines (accessed on July 15, 2004).

Hazen, Don. "Moving On: A New Kind of Peace Activism." *AlterNet* (February 11, 2003). http://www.alternet.org/story/15163 (accessed on July 15, 2004).

Heilemann, John. "Looking for Democracy's Next Big Thing." *Business 2.0* (July 2004). http://www.business2.com/b2/web/articles/0,17863, 655745,00.html (accessed on July 15, 2004).

Markels, Alex. "Virtual Peacenik." *Mother Jones* (May/June 2003). http://www.motherjones.com/news/hellraiser/2003/05/ma_379_01.html (accessed on July 15, 2004).

McNally, Terrence. "MoveOn as an Instrument of the People." *AlterNet* (June 25, 2004). http://www.alternet.org/story/19043 (accessed on July 19, 2004).

MoveOn Web site: Democracy in Action. MoveOn.org. http://www.move on.org (accessed on July 15, 2004).

Salerno, Heather. "Eli Pariser May Be Only 23, But He's Helping Change the Nation's Political Panorama." *Journal News (Westchester, New York)* (April 18, 2004). http://www.commondreams.org/headlines 04/0418-02.htm (accessed on July 15, 2004).

Tom Brady

Cy Cyr/WireImage.com.

August 3, 1977 • San Mateo, California

Football player

By the mid-2000s Tom Brady was the undisputed king of the grid-iron. In 2002 he became the youngest quarterback in the history of the National Football League (NFL) to lead his team to a Super Bowl victory. Two years later, in 2004, he proved the magic was still strong when he led the New England Patriots to their second Super Bowl title in three years. In addition, Brady was named the Super Bowl's Most Valuable Player (MVP) in 2002 and 2004. The dimpled, clean-cut quarterback had reached career heights that most veteran football players envied, and he had done it all before he was thirty years old.

Football, football, and more football

Thomas Edward Patrick Brady Jr. was born on August 3, 1977, in San Mateo, California, the youngest child, and only son, of Galynn and Tom Brady. The Bradys were a close-knit family, and they were all sports enthusiasts. The three Brady girls (Maureen, Nancy, and Julie) played every sport imaginable, including softball, soccer, and basketball. Tommy, as his family calls him, always went to their games and cheered them on. He also caught their competitive spirit. As Julie Brady explained to *People Weekly,* "We used to compete for absolutely everything, and we pushed [Tom] all the time." The nightly battles to control the television remote were especially fierce, and frequently the fighting took place with water pistols.

Brady's interest in football started when he was very young. Some of his earliest memories are of attending San Francisco 49ers games with his family every Sunday when the team was in town. "The Niners were my team," enthused Brady in a *CBS Under the*

> **"**Football has so many elements of sports. It's strength, and it's speed, and it's quickness. It's endurance. It's toughness. It's so fast. It's a great game to watch. It's a great game to play.**"**

Helmet interview. Brady was a particular fan of San Francisco quarterbacks Joe Montana (1956–) and Steve Young (1961–). When not going to football games, or watching football on television, Brady was playing football. While attending St. Gregory's elementary school in San Mateo (where he was an altar boy), he played flag football and touch football at recess and after school. His position? Quarterback.

Brady first played organized football as a freshman at San Mateo's Junipero Serra High School, a Catholic all-boys school. By his junior year he was a starting quarterback, and by his senior year he was being noticed by college and pro scouts. During Brady's high school quarterback career, he completed 236 of 447 passes (52.8 percent) for 3,702 yards, and thirty-one touchdowns. The multi-talented Brady was also a star catcher on the school's baseball team, and, when he graduated from high school in 1995, he was recruited to play pro-

I'm Going to Disney World!

In February of 2004, just hours after leading the New England Patriots to their second Super Bowl victory, quarterback Tom Brady was whisked away to join a whirlwind of celebrations. Where was he going? As he told millions of fans who were watching their television screens, "I'm going *back* to Disney World."

Brady joined a long line of athletes who have been featured in one of television's most famous advertising campaigns. In the ad, immediately following the game, a narrator asks, "You've just won the Super Bowl! What are you going to do next?" The player responds, "I'm going to Disney World!" The first ad, which aired in 1987, focused on Phil Simms (1955–), quarterback for the New York Giants, winners of Super Bowl XXI. The "What's next?" commercials became so famous that the phrase "I'm going to Disney World" became a part of American pop culture.

In 2004 Brady was going back to Disney World because he had already been there following his first Super Bowl win in 2002. Only three other NFL players have been featured twice in the commercials: Joe Montana (1956–), Emmitt Smith (1969–), and John Elway (1960–). Many of the players, like Brady, are MVPs, but not all. As Disney senior vice president of marketing Ken Potrock explained on PR Newswire, "We select players based on success in the field and a Cinderella-type story."

Brady definitely fit the bill. In both 2002 and 2004, he led his team to a storybook finish, so what better way to celebrate than with a fairy-tale ending. On February 2, the fairytale came true. Just one day after his Super Bowl win, Brady and his mother were riding through the streets of Disney's Magic Kingdom and thousands of fans, including Mickey Mouse, cheered the latest Super Bowl hero.

fessional baseball for the Montreal Expos. Instead, he opted to accept a scholarship to play football for the University of Michigan (U of M), in Ann Arbor.

Life as a Wolverine

During his first two years as a U of M Wolverine, Brady warmed the bench as a backup quarterback for future NFL stars Brian Griese (1975–) and Scott Driesbach (1975–). He was frustrated by his lack of play, and at one point, considered transferring back to California. However, Brady stuck it out, and in 1998, his junior year, he earned the starting quarterback position. He went on to earn an All–Big Ten Conference honorable mention; he was an Academic All–Big Ten Pick (he had a 3.3 grade point average); and he set several University of Michigan records, including the record for most attempts (350) and completions (214) in one season. Brady also led the Wolverines to

victory at the Citrus Bowl in 1999 and was named team co-captain the same year. In 2000 he became team captain.

Despite his success, Brady faced a setback his senior year when he was forced to share his quarterbacking duties with teammate Drew Henson (1980–). Henson was only a freshman, but he had been highly recruited in both football and baseball, and Wolverine coach Lloyd Carr feared that if not played, Henson might leave U of M in favor of a pro baseball career. Brady worked all the harder and completed the year by throwing the twenty-five-yard pass that brought victory to U of M over the University of Alabama in the 2000 Orange Bowl. The Orange Bowl, like the Citrus Bowl is a post-season competition between two college football teams. The four most prestigious bowl games are the Orange Bowl, the Cotton Bowl, the Sugar Bowl, and the Rose Bowl. Bowl games are always played as close as possible to New Year's Day.

By the time his college career came to a close, Brady had won twenty of the twenty-five games he started. He had arm strength and throwing accuracy, and he believed his chances were good for being chosen to play professional ball during the 2000 NFL draft. Things did not turn out as Brady hoped, however. During the draft he was the 199th player chosen, and he was picked up by the struggling New England Patriots. According to sports analysts, coaches were leery of Brady. They questioned his speed, but mostly they wondered why Henson, a freshman, had received so much playing time at the University of Michigan over the more seasoned senior. Brady showed up at the Patriot's training camp determined to prove himself. His U of M coach expected nothing less. "The more he gets knocked down," Carr commented to *People Weekly,* "the harder he competes. You can't underestimate Tom."

Stirs up a tired team

Although he was a fourth-string Patriot quarterback, Brady did not complain. Instead he watched and studied and prepared. He learned the Patriot playbook front to back, and he hit the weight room to bulk up his six-foot-four-inch frame from 204 to 220 pounds. He also pelted veteran teammates with questions about ways to improve his on-field strategy. By the end of his first season, Brady had played in only one game, during which he completed one pass. The game was against the Detroit

Lions, and the Patriots lost 34 to 9. The team ended the season at the very bottom of the AFC East division with a record of five wins and eleven losses. The thirty-two football teams that are part of the NFL are divided evenly into two conferences: the American Football Conference (AFC) and the National Football Conference (NFC). Within each conference, there are four divisions: North, South, East, and West.

During the off-season, Brady continued to work on improving his game, and at the 2001 training camp he was one of the team's most improved players. Brady so impressed his coaches that he was named back-up to the Patriot's star quarterback, Drew Bledsoe (1972–). On September 23, 2001, during the second game of the season, Bledsoe received a stunning blow to his chest, and barely made it off the field. A jittery Brady, who had not expected to play, stepped in to finish the game, which the Patriots ended up losing.

With Bledsoe out of commission, it seemed that the Patriots were doomed to face another losing season. However, as Brady began to get comfortable in his new role, things began to change. "I'm a big fan of Drew's," former Patriot safety Lawyer Milloy (1973–) told Michael Silver of *Sports Illustrated,* "but it was obvious the team needed something different, and Tom brought that youthful energy." With the calm confidence of someone much older than his twenty-four years, Brady helped the Patriots rack up a string of wins. In 2000 they finished at the bottom of the heap; in 2001 they were AFC Division champions, and they were going to the Super Bowl.

Packs a Patriot punch at the Super Bowl

The Super Bowl is the top competition in football, played each year between the two teams who are leaders from the AFC and NFC divisions. It has become a major television event that is watched by millions of fans throughout the world. Going into the Super Bowl, the New England Patriots were considered the underdogs, even though they ended the 2001 season with eleven wins and five losses. For one thing, their Super Bowl track record was not good. They had only competed twice, and they lost both times. Plus they were being led by an inexperienced quarterback: Tom Brady. The St. Louis Rams were the hands-down favorite to win Super Bowl XXXVI, scheduled for February 3, 2002.

Regardless of the predictions, Brady was so calm before the big game that he took a nap in the locker room. "When I woke up," Brady explained to Dave Kindred of *The Sporting News,* "I told myself it's a football game. It just comes down to playing football. I felt calm and confident." Brady's confidence was key since the game turned out to be a nail-biting battle. When the Rams tied things up with only one minute, thirty-nine seconds to go, people expected the game to go into overtime. Brady, however, set up a spectacular nine-play drive that positioned the Patriots for a field goal. With mere seconds left on the clock, the Patriots defeated the Rams, 20 to 17.

The Super Bowl win was only the beginning of Brady's Cinderella story. He not only led his team to victory, he was also named MVP of the game, and he set a new record as the youngest quarterback to win a Super Bowl at twenty-four years and 184 days old. One of the previous record-holders was his childhood idol, Joe Montana. In addition, Brady emerged as a true leader of his team, earning the respect of his coaches, teammates, and the sports press. According to sportswriter Paul Attner, "he has embraced his position with a passion and intelligence rarely seen in the game." Analyst Phil Simms of CBS noted that Brady "really knows how to play quarterback, how to interact with teammates, when to be their friend, when to be their leader and when to be their enemy when he has to. He can influence an entire franchise."

Sweet repeat

After the thrill of the Super Bowl, the following season was disappointing for the Patriots, and they did not make the playoffs. A determined Brady, however, rallied his team in 2003. The season started off slow with two wins and two losses, but then Brady and the Patriots took off on a winning streak. After winning fourteen games in a row, they were headed, once again, to the Super Bowl.

Super Bowl XXXVIII, played on February 1, 2004, was a memorable match-up between the Patriots and the Carolina Panthers. The first half was agonizingly long as both teams fought hard to control the field. At half-time, the score stood at Patriots 14, Panthers 10. The second half of the game proved to be a humdinger. The two teams scored a combined 37 points in the fourth quarter, and with four seconds left on the clock, New England's Adam Vinatieri made a forty-

Tom Brady of the New England Patriots, during a 2003 game against the Buffalo Bills. AP/Wide World Photos. Reproduced by permission.

one-yard field goal to win the game, 32 to 29. For the second time in three years, the underdog Patriots took home the championship.

For Brady, it was a sweet repeat. His game statistics were impressive: thirty-two completions in forty-eight attempts for 354 yards, and three touchdowns. He was named, once again, Most Valuable Player, and he broke another record by becoming, at age twenty-six, the youngest quarterback to win two Super Bowls.

Brady-mania

After his first Super Bowl win, Brady-mania swept the United States. Sportscasters could not heap enough praise on him, calling him meticulous, conscientious, and self-assured. Girls everywhere thought he was dreamy. Parents liked him, too. According to fellow teammate Larry

Izzo, who spoke with reporter Michael Silver, "Every mother and father in New England wants their daughter to be dating Tom Brady."

It seemed everyone was clamoring for the fresh-faced quarterback. Brady was a judge for the Miss USA Pageant; his face beamed down from billboards for the famous "Got Milk?" ad campaigns; and he was named one of *People* magazine's "50 Most Beautiful People of 2002." Just before his second Super Bowl, Brady was even invited to be a special guest at the White House for President George W. Bush's January of 2004 State of the Union address.

Brady seems to be handling his celebrity status with the same cool approach he has toward playing football. As he told Silver in *Sports Illustrated*, "Look, I'm a football player, and when I think back to the Miss USA pageant and all the other cool stuff I've done these last few weeks, the most fun I've had by far was winning the Super Bowl.... I know how I got here, and I'm going to devote myself to helping my team win it all again."

In addition, throughout it all, Brady has remained very close to his family, and perhaps it is thanks to them that he stays grounded. In an interview with Brady's hometown newspaper, the *San Mateo County Times*, Tom Brady Sr. put his son's celebrity into perspective: "Tommy's a hometown boy and, generally, everybody likes to see the hometown boy succeed."

For More Information

Books

Lazenby, Roland, and Bob Schron. *Tom Brady: Sudden Glory.* Chicago: Triumph Books, 2002.

Stewart, Mark. *Tom Brady: Heart of the Huddle.* Brookfield, CT: Millbrook Press, 2003.

Periodicals

Attner, Paul. "Brady's Bunch: Super Bowl Preview." *The Sporting News* (January 26, 2004): p. 16.

Chadiha, Jeff. "The Brady Hunch." *Sports Illustrated* (February 13, 2002): p. 46.

Fraley, Malaika. "Brady's Bunch: Neighbors, Family Bask in 'Tommy's' Football Glory." *The San Mateo County Times* (January 30, 2004).

Kindred, Dave. "A Day of Red, White, and Blue—and Brady." *The Sporting News* (February 11, 2002): p. 64.

King, Peter. "These Kids Can Play." *Sports Illustrated* (November 11, 2002): p. 36.

Silver, Michael. "Cool Customer: Fresh off a Storybook Season in Which He Quarterbacked the Patriots to a Super Bowl Victory at Age 24, Tom Brady Is Learning to Cope with the Blitz of Newfound Fame." *Sports Illustrated* (April 15, 2002): p. 34.

Tresniowski, Alex. "Super Cool Super Hero: A Benchwarmer Just Last Year, Patriots Quarterback Tom Brady Proves Too Good for the Rams—and Almost Too Good to Be True." *People Weekly* (February 18, 2002): p. 54.

Web sites

"Back in the Day with Tom Brady." Interview transcript. *CBS Under the Helmet* (August 31, 2002) http://images.nfl.com/partners/aol/index.html?http://www.nfl.com/reebok/bid/tbrady.html (accessed on May 31, 2004).

"Tom Brady biography." *Official Web site of the New England Patriots.* http://www.patriots.com/team/personal.sps?playerid=566&playertype=1&image4.x=11&image4.y=7 (accessed on May 31, 2004).

Larry Brown

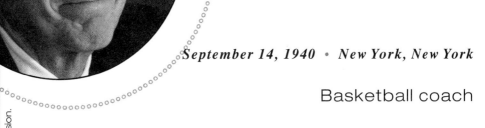

September 14, 1940 • *New York, New York*

Basketball coach

Many experts consider Larry Brown to be the best coach in the National Basketball Association (NBA). In Brown's case, that ranking is based not on the number of championship teams he has coached—the native New Yorker has led just one team to an NBA championship—but on his skill as a rebuilder of teams. Never staying long in one place, Brown would, in the words of *Sports Illustrated*'s Gary Smith, "come, conquer, and leave." As of 2004, Brown had coached ten college and professional teams in thirty-two years of coaching. In nearly every case, at least in the NBA, he came on board to convert a losing team into a winning one, developing the abilities of key players, pushing the concept of working as a team, and establishing a sense of the team as family.

At the end of the 2002–03 season, when Brown announced he would be leaving his post as coach of the Philadelphia 76ers, NBA franchises all over the country began to dream of luring Coach Brown to their teams. The victors in this contest were the Detroit Pistons, a team that strayed from the typical Larry Brown coaching project. The Pistons were not down and out; they had won fifty games and the division title for two seasons prior to Brown's arrival. But the management team in Detroit was hungry for a championship, and they felt certain that Brown could take them there. Brown did not disappoint. In just one season, he helped the Pistons go from being a strong team to being an unstoppable machine, beating the mighty Los Angeles Lakers four games to one, to win the NBA championship series. *Time* magazine called the victory "the sport's biggest upset in more than 25 years."

> **"**All I ask is that we play the game the right way. I want us to play as a team, share the ball, play unselfishly, defend and rebound every night, and respect the game.**"**

A painful childhood

Born in New York in 1940, Lawrence Harvey Brown was the second child born to Ann and Milton Brown. In a 2001 *Sports Illustrated* article, Ann described Larry when he was a child: "He was an angel, so quiet and gentle." When Brown was six years old, his father, then just forty-three years old, died suddenly. Fearing his reaction, Ann decided not to immediately tell her younger child that his father had died. Brown was sent to a relative's house for several weeks. When he asked about his father he was told that Milton, a traveling salesman, was on the road, working. A month later the boy learned the truth that he had suspected for many days, but he and his mother never spoke about it. To support the family, Ann went to work, spending long hours in the family's bakery in Long Beach, on Long Island, New York. Larry and his brother Herb occupied themselves playing basketball.

Brown graduated from Long Beach High School, where he was a standout basketball player. At the insistence of his future coach, Frank McGuire, Brown spent part of a year at a military academy to learn discipline and gain maturity, before enrolling at the University of North Carolina (UNC). There, coached by McGuire and Dean Smith, Brown and his teammates practiced the fundamentals over and over again. They were taught more than just skills, however: their coaches also drilled the players on style and attitude, encouraging them to treat each other with respect and to play unselfishly rather than try to be a superstar. Brown adopted these standards as his own, employing them later in his coaching jobs. After three seasons of playing varsity basketball at UNC, averaging a team-leading 16.2 points per game during his junior year, Brown graduated in 1963. He was invited to play for the U.S. basketball team in the 1964 Olympics, held in Tokyo, Japan. Brown and the rest of the team won nine games and lost none during the Olympics, returning home with the gold medal.

Here, there, and everywhere

During 1967 Brown began playing professional basketball for the newly formed American Basketball Association (ABA), a league that lasted just nine seasons. Brown played in the ABA on five different teams over five seasons. He made the ABA All-Star team three times, and in 1968 he was named the most valuable player (MVP) of the All-Star game. The following year Brown helped his team, the Oakland Oaks, win the ABA championship. After leaving the ABA as a player in 1972, Brown returned to the league one year later as head coach of the Carolina Cougars. He spent two years coaching the Cougars before moving to Denver to lead the Nuggets, a team that began as part of the ABA. Later, after the ABA folded, the team became part of the NBA. For each of his three seasons coaching in the ABA, Brown was named coach of the year. In 1979 he left the Nuggets and professional basketball and took a job coaching college basketball.

Brown's first job with the National Collegiate Athletic Association (NCAA) was coaching the Bruins at the University of California at Los Angeles. During his first season with the Bruins, Brown led the team to the NCAA championship game. While the Bruins did not win the big game, they did come up with forty-two wins against just seventeen losses during Brown's two seasons as coach. In 1981 Brown briefly returned to the NBA, coaching the New Jersey Nets to two winning seasons before heading back to the NCAA in 1983 to lead the Jayhawks at the

A Victory for the Underdogs

Even after the Detroit Pistons beat the Milwaukee Bucks, the New Jersey Nets, and the Indiana Pacers during the 2004 playoffs, few sportswriters outside of Detroit felt the Pistons had a chance to go all the way against the Los Angeles Lakers. Boasting the star power of Kobe Bryant and Shaquille O'Neal, not to mention the impressive winning streak of coach Phil Jackson—with nine NBA championships under his belt—the Lakers seemed to have every advantage. Sports commentators spoke of the depth of the Lakers' bench, the abundance of talent that went beyond the team's starting lineup. They pointed out that while the Pistons had perhaps the best defensive team in the NBA, their offense was inconsistent. Before the start of the finals, Ron Rapoport, columnist for the *Chicago Sun-Times,* asked, "Are these NBA Finals absolutely necessary? Can't we just declare the season over and tell the Lakers they can start their parade whenever they like?" He went on to describe the Pistons-Lakers series as "a disaster in the making" and an "ugly mismatch."

It turned out Rapoport was half right—in the end it did seem that the series was mismatched, but in Detroit's favor, not that of Los Angeles. Boasting a solid all-around team but no superstars, Detroit played with an energy and intensity that the Lakers could not match. In the first game, the Pistons displayed the defensive strategies they had become known for. Bryant and O'Neal both had high-scoring games, but as for the rest of the team, no Laker scored more than five points. The Pistons emerged victorious, 87-75. Game two looked like it might be a

University of Kansas (KU). Brown spent five seasons at KU, with his career there culminating in an NCAA championship in 1988.

Brown went back to the NBA for the 1988–89 season to coach the San Antonio Spurs. During his first year in Texas, the Spurs won only twenty-one games. The following two seasons, with Brown at the helm, they won more than fifty. Brown then moved on, heading west to Los Angeles to coach the Clippers for two seasons. In 1993 he became the head coach of the Indiana Pacers, leading the team to more victories than any coach had done before. The Pacers made it to the playoffs during three of Brown's four seasons there, and reached the finals twice.

Brown left Indiana in 1997 to take a job with the Philadelphia 76ers, then the worst team in the NBA. Brown spent a longer time in Philadelphia than he had anywhere else—six seasons—taking the team to heights they had not reached in many years. Brown took the 76ers to the playoffs for five straight seasons, becoming the first coach in the history of the NBA to reach the playoffs with six differ-

repeat performance, until Bryant pulled off a last-minute three-pointer to tie the game and send it into overtime. With the wind taken out of their sails, the Pistons petered out and the Lakers won, 99-91. Sports analysts declared that the psychological toll of losing game two would significantly damage the Pistons' chances in game three, even though that game would mark their return to their home stadium in Auburn Hills, Michigan. Once again, the Pistons defied expectations, blowing the Lakers away in an 88-68 victory. In an article in *Sports Illustrated,* Jack McCallum related a comment from the Lakers' Derek Fisher after the game three loss: "Their desire to be champions is greater than ours at this point."

Suddenly, it seemed that the Pistons might have a chance after all. Predictions favoring Detroit began to spread. During game four, O'Neal displayed the qualities that made him a star, scoring thirty-six points and grabbing twenty rebounds for the Lakers. Bryant, however, seemed to be trying too hard. McCallum wrote: "The worse he shot, the more he forced shots; the more he forced shots, the more he tried to make up for it." Bryant made only eight of twenty-five shots. The Pistons plowed on, winning 88-80. No team in NBA history had come back from a three-to-one deficit in the finals; the odds were in the Pistons' favor. The Lakers started with a bang in game five, taking a 14-7 lead in the first quarter. Following a strategic timeout, the Pistons charged onto the court, dominating the Lakers for the remainder of the quarter. At that point, wrote McCallum, "It was over. There were thirty-six minutes to play. But it was over." All five of the Pistons starters scored in double digits in game five, with center Ben Wallace collecting twenty-two rebounds. When the buzzer sounded, the Pistons had 100 points, the Lakers 87. For the first time in fourteen years, the Pistons were the NBA champs.

ent teams. The 76ers won fifty-six games during the 2000–01 season, the most victories they had had in more than fifteen years. That year the team made it to the finals, bringing Brown the closest he had come so far to an NBA championship. The road to greatness with the 76ers was a rocky one, with Brown thinking many times about quitting. He struggled with the team's star player, Allen Iverson, a talented and intense player who initially resisted Brown's authority and refused to cooperate—or sometimes even show up—at practices. But Brown persisted, and developed a trusting relationship with Iverson, pushing him to realize his potential and become a true team player. Iverson acknowledged the depth of their relationship to *Sports Illustrated*'s Gary Smith in 2001: "We've both learned a lot about basketball and life. I know one thing. Coach's voice will never leave my head as long as I live." Brown was named NBA Coach of the Year after the 2000–01 season, and the following year he was inducted into the Naismith Memorial Basketball Hall of Fame. He also added another Olympic gold medal to his collection, this time as the assistant coach for the 2000 U.S. team in Sydney, Australia.

Larry Brown confers with Pistons team members during a break in their 2004 game against the New Jersey Nets. AP/Wide World Photos. Reproduced by permission.

Brown's ups and downs

Throughout his many years of coaching, Brown has steadily and consistently taken teams that were fumbling and converted them into sleek, powerful, winning franchises. Brown views his role as that of teacher, and he has the patience to work exhaustively on improving players' skills. His way of teaching basketball, which he frequently refers to as "the right way," involves an intense, aggressive defensive style, with players giving it their all from the initial tip-off to the final buzzer. He demands a great deal from his players, giving in return his encouragement and confidence. Brown has shown an impressive ability to bring a sense of family to the teams he coaches. Greg Popovich, an NBA coach who served as assistant to Brown during his time with the San Antonio Spurs, told *Investor's Business Daily,* "Coach Brown truly does care about people. He wants to know what makes people tick—why they might be depressed on a certain day, who needs love, those sorts of things." His efforts to build his basketball families have cost him relationships in his personal life, however. Brown has been divorced twice and in the past endured years of barely speaking to his brother Herb. And as close as his relationships to his players become, they are always short-lived, with Brown leaving his post every few years, always seemingly on the hunt for the perfect situation.

When he announced his decision to leave the 76ers in the spring of 2003, Joe Dumars—former star player and current general manager of the Detroit Pistons—did not hesitate to call Brown. Dumars was not sure the Pistons would appeal to Brown. As Sean Deveney put it in an article at *FOXSports.com,* "Brown's reputation was akin to St. Jude, the patron saint of hopeless causes. He was a guy who came in, fixed a broken team, and moved on to the next broken team." And the Pistons were not exactly a broken team. Dumars felt certain, however, that Brown would be attracted to the Pistons' potential to go all the way—with a little help from a respected teacher and devoted coach. Brown accepted Dumars's offer and headed to the suburbs of Detroit.

Detroit basketball

For the players, the transition to working with Brown is not always an easy one. Zeroing in on exactly what will make each player better, Brown works with the players relentlessly to bring them to his standards. He insists that their habits and attitudes change to conform to his model of the "right way" to play basketball. At the same time, he earns the players' respect and loyalty, reaching the point where his goals become their goals. The Pistons were a good team before Brown came on board, but throughout the 2003–04 season they steadily improved. The team really jelled with the acquisition of six-foot-eleven-inch power forward Rasheed Wallace in February of 2004. His abilities on both offense and defense provided the force the Pistons needed to move to the next level of play. In the month of March, the Pistons won eight straight games by fifteen or more points, an NBA record. They made the record books again when they held their opponents to less than seventy points for five games in a row.

During playoff season the Pistons defied expectations by plowing through their opponents. First they defeated the Milwaukee Bucks in the first round, four games to one. Then, over seven games against the New Jersey Nets, the Pistons squeezed out a victory in the Eastern Conference semifinals. The Pistons then claimed the Eastern Conference championship with a four-games-to-two victory over the Indiana Pacers. Next up: the NBA finals, with the Pistons pitted against the seemingly unstoppable Los Angeles Lakers. The Lakers were heavily favored, placing the Pistons squarely in underdog territory. Pacing the sidelines, Brown fretted over every missed shot, every turnover, every lost rebound. In the end, Brown and the Pistons were victorious, beating Los Angeles in five games. Brown became the only coach in history to win both an NCAA and an NBA championship.

At the beginning of the 2003 basketball season, *Sporting News* reported the results of a poll of NBA general managers. In the categories of best coach for developing young players and best overall head coach, Larry Brown earned the most votes. In thirty-two years as a head coach—with the NCAA, the now-defunct ABA, and the NBA—Brown has led his teams to a winning season, winning more games than were lost, twenty-eight times. When he was first hired to lead the Pistons, a journalist asked the restless sixty-three-year-old coach if Detroit would be his final coaching job before retirement. Brown replied, according to *Sports Illustrated*'s Richard Deitsch, "This will be my last stop." In response, Deitsch quoted fellow writer Gary Smith as saying: "Somehow I don't think so.… But there is one thing I'm sure of: Somewhere, somehow, Larry Brown will [always] be a coach."

For More Information

Periodicals

Deitsch, Richard. "He Keeps Going and Going." *Sports Illustrated* Championship Edition (June 30, 2004): p. 87.

Deveney, Sean. "A Worthy Challenger." *Sporting News* (April 12, 2004): p. 36.

Gregory, Sean. "Motown Masterminds." *Time* (June 28, 2004): p. 62.

McCallum, Jack. "The Rise of the Working Class." *Sports Illustrated* Championship Edition (June 30, 2004): p. 47.

McCosky, Chris. "What Will Brown Do to You?" *Sporting News* (October 27, 2003): p. 20.

Mink, Michael. "Champion Coach Larry Brown." *Investor's Business Daily* (June 28, 2004): p. A07.

Rapoport, Ron. "Forgettable NBA Finals Need Fast, Merciful Ending." *Chicago Sun-Times* (June 3, 2004).

Smith, Gary. "Mama's Boys." *Sports Illustrated* (April 23, 2001): p. 54.

Smith, Gary. "'Where You Gonna Be Next Year, Larry?'" *Sports Illustrated* (November 12, 1984): p. 106.

Web Sites

Deveney, Sean. "Brown, Pistons a Good Fit." *FOXSports.com.* http://msn.foxsports.com/content/view?contentId=2490118 (accessed on July 1, 2004).

"Larry Brown." *HoopHall.com: Official Website of the Basketball Hall of Fame.* http://www.hoophall.com/halloffamers/brown_larry.htm (accessed on June 29, 2004).

"Larry Brown." *NBA.com* http://www.nba.com/coachfile/larry_brown/ (accessed on June 30, 2004).

Mark Burnett

July 17, 1960 • *London, England*

Television producer

In May 2000, when Americans first heard the phrase "the tribe has spoken," television as we knew it changed forever. The speaker was host Jeff Probst; the television show was *Survivor*; the show's creator was British-born producer Mark Burnett. *Survivor* was a game show like no other before it. With sixteen castaways battling to win a million-dollar prize on a deserted island, it was part athletic competition and part soap opera. Millions tuned in to watch the contestants experience conditions of deprivation, dilemma, and physical challenge. The savvy Burnett realized that the audience watching this show was the key to a gold mine, and he soon began work on other reality television series. In 2003 he produced *The Restaurant,* which presented the ups and downs that go into launching a new restaurant. In 2004 Burnett's "The Apprentice" drew millions of viewers as contestants vied to win a corporate position with one of America's richest businessmen. Along the way, Burnett became one of the most powerful men in Hollywood, and everyone watched as he earned the title, "king of reality TV."

From commando to nanny

Mark Burnett came from a humble, but very supportive family. He was born in July 17, 1960, in London, England's East End to parents who were factory workers. His father worked in a Ford Motor Company plant; his mother worked in the battery compound next door. Although the Burnetts could not afford to give their only child a lot of material things, they did give him plenty of encouragement. Burnett's mother, in particular, served as an early role model. As Burnett recalled in his autobiography *Dare to Succeed*, "She always dressed immaculately, never letting her station in life interfere with how she presented herself." She passed that sense of pride on to her son, and

> **"I heard my name associated with the Peter Pan syndrome more than once. But, really, what's so wrong with Peter Pan? Peter Pan flies. He is a metaphor for dreams and faith."**

always explained to him that he could achieve anything in life he wanted. She was also her son's biggest champion. Burnett explained in his autobiography, "Basically, she supported every crazy thing I had ever done my whole life."

When he was seventeen years old, Burnett joined the British Army. In a short time, he became a section commander of the prestigious Parachute Regiment. Burnett saw active duty in Northern Ireland and the Falkland Islands, and left the army in 1982 a decorated soldier. Although he observed the horrors of war, Burnett also had his first taste of adventure, a taste that would stay with him the rest of his life.

Not sure what to do after the service, Burnett decided to take a position as a military adviser in Central America. He did not tell his mother the full details, only that he was taking a "security job." Burnett's mother told him she had an uneasy feeling about the job, and she asked her son to reconsider accepting it. When he landed in Los Angeles, in 1982, on his way to Central America, Burnett thought about his mother's warning and decided to stay put in the United States. With $600 in his pocket, he contemplated his next move. A friend of his who was living in Los Angeles told him about a wealthy Malibu family who was looking for a nanny. Impressed by his cleaning and ironing abilities (learned in the strict British Army environment), Burnett was hired.

The commando-turned-nanny worked for two different families over the course of several years. Burnett became lifelong friends with one of his employers (named Burt), and Burt eventually developed into the young man's mentor. Burnett quizzed the producers and businessmen he came into contact with through Burt, and he soaked up all the information they could offer. Eventually, Burt hired Burnett to sell insurance. During the late 1980s, Burnett went from selling insurance to selling T-shirts along a fence in Venice Beach, California, to starting his own marketing and advertising firm. By the early 1990s, the English immigrant who had come to the United States with a few hundred dollars had earned his first million. By all accounts, he was a success. However, Burnett felt something was missing. That something was adventure.

Eco-Challenge

In February 1991, Burnett found his inspiration. While flipping through the *Los Angeles Times* he happened upon an article describing a French adventure competition called the Raid Gauloises. Each year, five-person teams from various countries competed in an exotic location for up to two weeks. The race was grueling as team members competed nonstop, taking on such tasks as marathon kayaking, horseback riding (or even camel-riding, depending on the location), and parachuting. Such physically demanding competitions were not new to Europe, but the United States had nothing of the kind. Burnett decided to fix that. He would create his own competition, call it Eco-Challenge, and produce it for American television.

Burnett felt he had to prepare for Eco-Challenge. As he remarked in his autobiography, "I took an unusual step. I would race in the Raid-Gauloises. This would show me how my future customers actually felt while racing, and help me become a better race producer." Burnett pulled together Team American Pride, the first U.S. team ever to compete in the Raid Gauloises. He and Team America compet-

Mark Burnett's Principles of Success

Mark Burnett is an inspiration story. From soldier to nanny; from salesman to producer, he is a true man of vision. As Kevin Downey of *Broadcasting & Cable* put it, "Burnett has a vision that strays far from the norm. Fortunately for him, advertisers and millions of viewers have turned some of his dreams into hits." According to Burnett, however, the keys to success are easy ones that everyone can follow. In his best-selling book *Dare to Succeed: How to Survive and Thrive in the Game of Life,* he describes seven principles that have been a guide "through the minefields dividing dreams and success."

1. Only results count.

2. Have the courage to fail.

3. Choose teammates wisely.

4. Perseverance produces character.

5. Be right or be wrong, but make a decision.

6. Set achievable goals.

7. Try to go above, beyond, and then further.

ed in the 1992 Raid in Oman, the 1993 Raid in Madagascar, and the 1994 Raid in Borneo. By 1995 Burnett was ready to launch his own race. He formed a management team, poured every cent he had into the idea (including taking a loan against his house), and pitched the idea to several television networks. On April 25, 1995, the first Eco-Challenge was held in Utah, and broadcast on MTV. The show later migrated to the Discovery Channel and then to the USA Network.

Billed as the "toughest race in the world," the first competition spanned over 370 miles across the rocky terrain of southern Utah, and included more than fifty teams. Players had to ride on horseback for 26 miles, swim in cold water carrying backpacks, and hike more than 100 miles across the desert. Some of the players did not make it and had to be flown by helicopter to safety. When an interviewer from *Boy's Life* asked Burnett why people would put themselves through such physical torture, he explained, "Only by taking people to their lowest low do they learn something about themselves."

Players kept coming back for more, and so did audiences. Burnett produced eight more Eco-Challenges, which took place in one exotic location after another, including Morocco (1998), Borneo (2000), New Zealand (2002), and Fiji (2003). *Eco-Challenge* was nominated several times for an Emmy award (the highest achievement in television) and received many top honors, including a 1996 Sports Emmy.

Survival of the fittest

Inspired by the success of *Eco-Challenge,* Burnett geared up to produce another competition-based series. During the course of the Eco-Challenge races, he was intrigued by how the players interacted with each other under stress. As he told *USA Today* online, "*Eco-Challenge* proved to me that the communication within groups was much more a factor in an expedition success than technical or physical attributes. And that's what attracted me to *Survivor.*"

Survivor was actually the brainchild of British producer Charlie Parsons. Burnett purchased the rights to the idea from Parsons in 1998. As he wrote in his autobiography, "I had a gut feeling that I could make this great concept even greater." It took Burnett a few years to convince networks of his gut feeling. Network after network turned down the project until 2000, when CBS snapped it up, hoping to air it during the empty summer months when its regular line-up was in reruns.

Six thousand people applied for the chance to be dropped off on a remote island in order to compete for food, shelter, and the ultimate prize of one million dollars. Only sixteen were chosen, ranging from Rudy, a retired Navy SEAL (a highly skilled military division), to a female truck driver named Susan. The men and women were divided into two "tribes," and over the course of thirty-nine days they competed in such challenges as fish-spearing, slug-eating, and running obstacle courses. At the end of each show, the losing team of the night met in tribal councils and voted off one of their own members.

Survivor was an immediate and outrageous success. Viewers flocked to their sets every Thursday night to find out who was voted off, and tuned in on Friday mornings to watch ousted tribal members interviewed on radio and TV talk shows. On August 23, 2000, over fifty million people tuned in to watch the series finale. The show's winner, Richard Hatch, became an instant celebrity; producer Mark Burnett became a multi-millionaire; and *Survivor* went down in pop culture history as the most successful reality show of all time.

From island jungle to concrete jungle

Burnett went on to create a number of *Survivor* sequels and specials, and although none quite reached the heights of the original, each

Mark Burnett (center) and the cast of Survivor: Pearl Island *pose with their 2004 People's Choice Award.* AP/Wide World Photos. Reproduced by permission.

attracted record numbers of viewers. In December 2003, when *Survivor: Pearl Island* (the seventh installment in the series) ended, it was the second-most watched program on network television. In May of 2004 more than twenty-four million viewers saw Amber Brkich named the winner of the *Survivor: All Stars* competition, which set eighteen past cast members in competition against one another.

In addition to its popularity with audiences, *Survivor* received praise from critics and was nominated for fourteen Emmy awards, winning two. Perhaps the real mark of success was that *Survivor* spawned a number of imitators, including *Big Brother* and *Joe Millionaire*. Such shows hoped to cash in on the reality craze, but none even came close.

Burnett was not yet finished riding the reality show wave. In 2003 he took his cameras to Oahu, Hawaii, and introduced viewers to the world of professional surfing in *Boarding House: North Shore*. He also gave us a behind-the-scenes look at the restaurant business while following up-and-coming New York chef Rocco DiSpirito in *The*

Restaurant. Neither show had quite the draw of *Survivor.* In 2004, however, Burnett moved from the island jungles to the concrete jungle in *The Apprentice.* And, once again, he hit the jackpot.

On the surface, *The Apprentice* sounded very much like *Survivor:* sixteen contestants picked to compete in a number of challenges to win a grand prize. In this case, the contestants were men and women with backgrounds in business, the playing field was set on the streets of New York City, and the winner got the chance to work for Donald Trump (1946–), a U.S. real estate whiz who is estimated to be worth approximately $4 billion. Burnett was a longtime fan of Trump, and in 2002 he got the chance to meet his idol when he leased the skating rink in Central Park for a *Survivor* finale. Trump owns the rink (as well as many other New York City landmarks), and the two got to talking. They both agreed that a competition set in New York would be perfect since, as Trump remarked to *Entertainment Weekly,* "New York City is the toughest jungle of them all."

Over the fifteen episodes, two teams (men versus women) competed to see who was the best at selling lemonade, designing ad campaigns, and renting high-priced apartments. At the end of each show, instead of gathering at a tribal council, the losing team met with Trump in the "boardroom." Just as millions tuned in to watch Jeff Probst extinguish a tribal member's torch, millions more tuned in to watch Trump flick his wrist, point at the losing player, and say, "You're fired!" By the series end, the contestants had again become celebrities, as fans rooted for the conniving Omarosa, mild-mannered Kwame, and spastic Sam; the network and Burnett were taking home barrels of cash; and Burnett cemented himself as the guru, the titan, the king of reality TV. Following the success of *The Apprentice,* Trump wrote in *Time* that "Burnett is a great visionary, able to see into the future with far better accuracy than any of his competitors. His No. 1 talent is having the right idea at the right time.... The positive impact of his efforts has been seen and felt by tens of millions of people."

King of unscripted drama

In interviews Burnett acknowledges that he has tapped into a new type of television producing, but he bristles at the term "reality TV." As he told Josh Mankiewicz of *Dateline NBC,* he prefers to call his creations, "unscripted dramas." Regardless of what they are called, there seems to be no end to them. In March 2004, Burnett launched a program called *Recovery,* which follows a CIA agent who recovers abducted children. Premiering in June 2004, *The Casino* follows two entrepreneurs who purchase the failing Golden Nugget Hotel and Casino in Las Vegas, Nevada, in the hopes of resurrecting its glory days. Burnett is also producing *The Contender,* along with actor-director Sylvester Stallone (1946–). The focus of the show is a nationwide search for the next boxing superstar.

By 2004, forty million people were watching Mark Burnett–produced shows every week on at least three major networks. He was also a best-selling author, a motivational speaker, and he appeared on almost every "who's who" list imaginable, from *"Entertainment Weekly's* Top 101 Most Powerful People in Entertainment" to *"TV Guide's* Most Valuable Players" list. In his spare time, Burnett was active in a number of charities, and he remained a top-notch athlete: he is a certified scuba diver and an advanced-level skydiver. What is Burnett's message to adventurers out there? As he told Josh Mankiewicz of *MSNBC,* "There's nothing like biting off more than you can chew and chew it anyway."

For More Information

Books

Burnett, Mark. *Dare to Succeed: How to Survive and Thrive in the Game of Life.* New York: Hyperion, 2001.

Periodicals

Armstrong, Jennifer. "Donald's Kids: Sixteen Go-Getters Will Do Anything to Land a Job with Trump." *Entertainment Weekly* (December 19, 2003): p. 64.

Boga, Steve. "Challenge of a Lifetime." *Boy's Life* (August 1996).

Downey, Kevin. "A Dreamer of Real Dreams: Burnett Launched a Television Genre and Has Seen It Gain Respect." *Broadcasting & Cable* (January 19, 2004) p. 10A).

Poniewozik, James. "The Art of the Real: Donald Trump Doesn't Hand Out Roses, But He Does Break Hearts on the Reality Showdown 'The Apprentice.'" *Time* (January 12, 2004): p. 69.

Trump, Donald J. "Mark Burnett: The Guru of Reality Television." *Time* (April 26, 2004): p. 95.

Web Sites

The Apprentice Web site. http://www.nbc.com/The_Apprentice (accessed on May 29, 2004).

Curtis, Bryan. "Mark Burnett: Saving the World One Reality Show at a Time." *MSN: Slate Web site* (April 12, 2004). http://slate.msn.com/id/2098688 (accessed on May 29, 2004)>

Mankiewicz, Josh. "Mark Burnett: Mr. Reality TV." *MSNBC: Dateline NBC* (April 16, 2004). http://www.msnbc.msn.com/id/4740184 (accessed on May 29, 2004).

Survivor Web site. http://www.cbs.com/primetime/survivor8/index.shtml (accessed on May 29, 2004).

"Survivor: Mark Burnett." *USA Today Online* (July 19, 2000). http://www.usatoday.com/community/chat/0719burnett.htm (accessed May 29, 2004).

Benjamin Solomon Carson

September 18, 1951 • Detroit, Michigan

Neurosurgeon, motivational speaker, philanthropist, author

Ben Carson is one of the most famous and respected doctors in the world. Since the 1980s, his surgeries to separate conjoined twins have made international headlines, and his pioneering techniques have revolutionized the field of neurosurgery. Almost as important is that Carson has become a role model for people of all ages, especially children. Although he works thirteen-hour days and performs hundreds of operations a year, Carson makes time to spread his message that anything in life is possible, regardless of what color a person is or where he is from. Carson speaks from experience. He went from the inner-city streets of Detroit, Michigan, to the halls of Yale University, to director of pediatric neurosurgery at one of the most prestigious hospitals in the United States. In 2004 Carson was awarded the Healthcare Humanitarian Award because he has "enhanced the quality of human lives … and has influenced the course of history through ongoing contributions to healthcare and medicine."

The "dumbest kid in the world"

Carson's mother, Sonya Copeland, was only thirteen years old when she married a much older Baptist minister from Tennessee named Robert Solomon Carson. After the couple moved to Detroit, Michigan, they had two boys, Curtis, born in 1949, and Benjamin Solomon, born on September 18, 1951. When young Ben was only eight years old, his parents divorced, and Sonya Carson was left to raise her two sons alone. Sonya moved the boys to Boston, Massachusetts, to be near family, but less than a year later the Carsons returned to Detroit. Sonya took on two, sometimes three, cleaning jobs at a time to support her children. In his writings, Carson has commented that even during the hardest times, his mother was the family's rock.

> "One of the things that really has inspired me and pushed me on is learning about the human brain and recognizing the incredible potential that lies there—but also recognizing how few people use it."

He was never a good student, but when Carson returned to his Michigan elementary school he realized that he was far behind the other fifth graders. In fact, in an *Oracle* interview with Andrew Pina, Carson recalled being laughed at by his classmates who, one day at recess, decided he was not only the dumbest kid in the fifth grade, but maybe the dumbest kid in the whole world. Life at Higgens Elementary was also not easy because it was a predominantly white school, and Carson, one of the few African American students, was taunted by his schoolmates and ignored by teachers.

Sonya Carson decided to take matters into her own hands by switching off the television. Ben and Curtis were allowed to watch only two programs a week, and their mother made them read two books each week from the Detroit Public Library. The boys were also

Carson Scholars

In 1994 Ben Carson and his wife, Candy, established the Carson Scholars Fund. Carson noticed that schools honored athletes with trophies and pep rallies, but that academic achievement often went unnoticed. He also wanted to encourage students to explore the fields of science and technology. According to the fund's Web site (http://www.carson-scholars.org), the goal of the nonprofit organization is to "to help our children stay competitive in science, math, and technology, as well as balance academic achievement with the high esteem our society gives to sports and entertainment.

Each year, scholarships of $1,000 are awarded to students in grades four through twelve who achieve a grade point average of at least 3.75, and who show a true commitment to their community. Scholarships are presented at an awards banquet where winners are also given certificates and medals. Currently, the program exists in Maryland, Washington, D.C., and Delaware. Certain cities in several other states, including Battle Creek, Michigan, also participate. The ulti-

mate goal of Dr. Carson, "is to have a Carson scholar in every school in the United States."

Proceeds from the sale of Carson's books help support the scholarship program, but in 2003 Carson found a different funding source. Directors Peter and Bobby Farrelly approached the famous physician about playing himself in their movie, *Stuck on You,* about conjoined adult twins who are separated. The movie was a comedy, and at first Carson was doubtful about becoming involved. However, when he read the script he actually liked it and realized the film was going to be tastefully done. As Carson told *U.S. News & World Report,* "they do give you some insights on what that must be like to be connected to someone 24-7." The rest of the Carsons also appeared in the movie: Candy was a nurse, and Carson's children played extras in the hospital waiting room. When the movie premiered in Baltimore, Maryland, home of Johns Hopkins, all the proceeds went to the Carson Scholars Fund and to the BEN Fund, which provides financial aid to children who cannot afford necessary surgeries.

required to write book reports, which Sonya would underline and mark up. Only later did Ben Carson realize his mother, who had left school after the third grade, was barely able to read. "She pulled a fast one on us," Carson told David Gergen of PBS, "but after a while, something happened. I began to actually enjoy reading the books.... I could go anywhere in the world, be anybody, do anything. You know my imagination began to run wild." Within a year-and-a-half Carson went from the bottom of his class to the top of his class.

Another obstacle that threatened to defeat Carson was his violent temper. Sometimes his anger was provoked, like when he was teased. Other times he lashed out over insignificant things. When he was fourteen, for example, Carson stabbed a friend because the boy had changed the radio station. This incident terrified Carson, who realized, as he told *Current Science,* that he was headed for "jail, reform school, or the grave." Carson turned to prayer, and learned to make peace with himself and others. Even today, the physician relies on his Christian faith, and prays before and after each surgery.

Brain power

By the time he graduated from Southwestern High School in 1969, Carson was earning all A's, and his classmates, who only a few years before called him the dumbest kid in school, voted him the most likely to succeed. He received a full scholarship to attend Yale University in New Haven, Connecticut, where, in 1973, he earned a bachelor's degree in psychology. From there, he headed back to Michigan to attend medical school. Carson had wanted to become a doctor since he was a boy, after hearing about medical missionaries in sermons at church. He originally planned to become a psychiatrist, but during his first year in medical school he was intrigued by the field of neurosurgery (surgery of the brain, nerves, and spinal cord).

After earning a medical degree from the University of Michigan in 1977, the young physician was accepted into the residency program in general surgery at the prestigious Johns Hopkins Hospital in Baltimore, Maryland. Carson was the hospital's first African American neurosurgical resident, and by 1982, he was the chief resident of neurosurgery. In 1983 Carson and his wife, Lacena "Candy" Rustin (whom he had met at Yale), moved to Perth, Australia, because Carson had been invited to be the chief neurosurgical resident at the Sir Charles Gairdner Hospital, one of Australia's leading centers for brain surgery. Because there were few neurosurgeons in the country, Carson gained a great deal of experience in a short time. As he wrote in his book *Gifted Hands,* "In my one year there I got so much surgical experience that my skills were honed tremendously, and I felt remarkably capable and comfortable working on the brain."

In 1984 Carson returned to the United States, and to Johns Hopkins, where at age thirty-three he was named director of pediatric (child) neurosurgery. He was the youngest doctor ever to hold the position, and Carson remains head of pediatric neurosurgery to this day. Carson quickly gained a reputation as a skillful surgeon; he also became known as someone who would take on cases that other doctors thought were risky or hopeless. In addition, Carson was eager to combine his own surgical skills and knowledge of the workings of the brain, with technology. As a result, he became a pioneer in advanced surgical methods.

Some of Carson's most difficult cases involved patients who suffered from chronic seizures (uncontrollable attacks that come from abnormal electrical discharges in the brain). In some cases, patients were having more than one hundred seizures a day. Carson revived a surgical procedure that had been abandoned because it was considered too dangerous. Called a hemispherectomy, the surgery involves removing half of a patient's brain. Carson performed his first successful hemispherectomy in 1985, and since then the operation has helped many patients lead healthy, normal lives.

Separating conjoined twins

Carson made numerous other advancements in neurosurgery. For example, he developed a new method to treat brain-stem tumors and was the first doctor to perform surgery on a fetus inside the womb. However, by the late 1980s, Carson became known as an expert in one of the most difficult types of surgeries: separating conjoined twins (identical twins born with connected body parts). Conjoined twins occur once in every seventy thousand to one hundred thousand births. Separating conjoined twins is difficult because they sometimes share internal organs or major blood vessels.

In 1987 Carson was called upon to separate two babies from Ulm, Germany, named Patrick and Benjamin Binder. The boys were *craniopagus* twins, which means they were joined at the head. Craniopagal joining is among the rarest forms of conjoined twins, occurring about once in every two million births. Because the condition is so rare and because one, or both, children usually die in surgery, most doctors were skeptical of the case. Carson, however, agreed to perform the surgery. Because the boys were joined at the back of the head, and because they had separate brains, he felt the operation could be performed successfully. Plus, as Carson told *Current Science,* "In my field, you take all comers."

Carson and his team of more than seventy people prepared for five months before the surgery, which included performing several dress rehearsals. On September 5, 1987, after twenty-two hours in the operating room, the boys were successfully separated. Part of the success was because Carson had developed a method to stop the flow of blood while he and other surgeons performed the delicate task of untangling, dividing, and repairing shared blood vessels. Although the twins suffered brain damage, both survived the operation and became the first craniopagus twins to successfully be separated.

In the 1990s Carson surgically separated two sets of craniopagus twins. The 1994 separation of the Makwaeba twins in South Africa was not successful; both girls died from complications of the surgery. In 1997, however, Carson and his team were able to separate Luka and Joseph Banda, infant boys from Zambia, in South Central Africa. Both boys survived, and neither one suffered severe brain damage. The Bandas were the first set of twins joined at the tops of their heads to be successfully surgically separated.

Laden (left) and Laleh Bijani, the Iranian conjoined twins Ben Carson and others operated on in an attempt to separate them. AP/ Wide World Photos. Reproduced by permission.

Adult separation

In 2003 Carson faced perhaps his biggest challenge: separating two adult conjoined twins. Ladan and Laleh Bijani, who were joined at the head, were twenty-nine years old when they decided to be separated. The separation of adult craniopagus twins had never been attempted because the outcome was almost certain to be death for both patients. Even Carson, ever the optimist, was not sure what the results would be. He tried to talk the two women out of the surgery, but after many discussions with them, he agreed to move forward. Ladan and Laleh had law degrees, were extremely bright and, according to Carson, they knew exactly what was in store for them. As Carson recounted to Andrew Pina, more than anything the women wanted to live independent lives: "They said, 'We would rather die than spend another day together.'"

Carson and a team of more than one hundred surgeons, specialists, and assistants conducted the fifty-two-hour operation on July 8, 2003, in Singapore (Southeast Asia). They used a 3-D imaging technique that Carson had developed for the Banda operation. The computerized images allowed the team to practice "virtually" before the operation and allowed them to follow a computerized reconstruction of the twins' brains during surgery. Midway through the operation, however, complications set in, and Ladan and Laleh both died because of severe blood loss. As devastating as the loss was, Carson told the press, as reported in the *Observer,* "What they have contributed to science will live far beyond them."

Medical superstar

People around the world were intrigued by conjoined twins, and Carson's surgeries generated a lot of press. At first, the soft-spoken doctor was known in the media only as a hospital spokesperson who explained complicated operations in terms that everyone could understand. Eventually, Carson's own story began to pique the interest of the public. Everyone was fascinated that such a "miracle worker" had come from such humble beginnings, and soon Carson became a motivational speaker, much in demand at schools, hospitals, and businesses. He traveled across the United States, explaining that if he was able to overcome such obstacles as poverty and racism, anyone could. On his Web site, Carson outlined what he believes to be the keys to success: "One's ability to discover his or her potential for excellence; the acquisition of knowledge to develop it; and a willingness to help others." The biggest key is education, which according to Carson, "leads to liberation."

In 2002 Carson was forced to cut back on his public appearances a bit when he faced a medical problem of his own. In June he was diagnosed with prostate cancer, but fortunately the cancer was caught in time. Carson the surgeon became Carson the patient, but that did not stop him from taking an active role in his own case. The feisty doctor reviewed his own X-rays and quizzed the team of surgeons who operated on him. Carson fully recovered from his surgery and came away with a clean bill of health.

Because of his brush with death, however, Carson made a few life changes. Although he was always interested in cancer, Carson told *Ebony,* now he is "looking more at root causes of cancer and how it can be prevented." He still operates on more than three hundred children a year, but he has been trying to shorten his days: prior to his cancer he used to work from 7:00 in the morning until 8:00 at night. Now, he tries to leave the hospital at 6:15 P.M. This gives him more time to spend with his wife and three children, Murray, Benjamin Jr., and Rhoeyce, and to indulge in his other passion, playing pool.

Carson still keeps up a busy speaking schedule, but children also visit him at Johns Hopkins to see their role model in person. In addition, Carson has written several books that recount his life story and encourage people everywhere to strive for excellence. Because of his unflagging commitment to children and his many medical breakthroughs, Carson has received countless awards and honorary degrees. In 2004 there was even talk of a Hollywood movie that would tell the world more about the man *Ebony* magazine called a "medical superstar."

For More Information

Books

Carson, Ben, with Cecil Murphey. *Gifted Hands.* Washington, DC: Review and Herald, 1990.

Carson, Ben, with Cecil Murphey. *Think Big: Unleashing Your Potential for Excellence.* Grand Rapids, MI: Zondervan, 1992.

Carson, Ben, with Gregg Lewis. *The Big Picture: Getting Perspective on What's Really Important in Life.* Grand Rapids, MI: Zondervan, 1999.

Periodicals

"Dr. Ben Carson: Top Surgeon's Life-and-Death Struggle with Prostate Cancer." *Ebony* (January 2003): p. 38.

Hallett, Vicky. "He Split Up Matt and Greg." *U.S. News & World Report* (December 15, 2003): p. 16.

McLaughlin, Sabrina. "Split Decisions: Surgeon Ben Carson Is a Master at Separating Conjoined Twins." *Current Science* (April 16, 2004).

Pina, Andrew. "A Look at 'The Big Picture.'" *The Oracle* (April 12, 2004).

Vaira, Douglas. "The Good Doctor: Dr. Benjamin Carson Proves That with Determination and Confidence, Anything Is Possible." *Association Management* (October 2003): pp. 56–61.

Web Sites

Dr. Ben Carson Web site. http://www.drbencarson.com (accessed on June 27, 2004).

Gergen, David. "The Big Picture: Interview with Dr. Ben Carson." *PBS Online NewsHour* (September 7, 1999). http://www.pbs.org/newshour/ gergen/july-dec99/carson_9-7.html (accessed June 27, 2004).

McKie, Robin. "Doctors 'Begged' Twins to Call Off Surgery." *Observer* (July 13, 2003). http://www.guardian.co.uk/iran/story/0,12858,997302, 00.html (accessed on June 26, 2004).

"Pediatric Neurosurgeon Benjamin Carson, M.D. to Separate Adult Con-joined Twins in Singapore." *Johns Hopkins Press Release* (June 12, 2003). http://www.hopkinsmedicine.org/press/2003/June/030612.htm (accessed on June 27, 2004.

Keisha Castle-Hughes

March 24, 1990 • Donnybrook, Western Australia

Actress

Steve Granitz/Wire Image.com.

Growing up in New Zealand, Keisha Castle-Hughes dreamed of someday becoming an actress, though she suspected that achieving such a goal would be extremely difficult. In 2001, when Castle-Hughes was just eleven years old, a casting director visited her school searching for a young girl to play the lead role in an upcoming movie. In a fairy-tale-like scenario, Castle-Hughes was awarded the role, chosen from among hundreds of children to play Pai, the main character in *Whale Rider.* Just three years later, in February of 2004, she found herself seated in one of the front rows of the Kodak Theatre in Los Angeles, California, at the seventy-sixth annual Academy Awards ceremony. Castle-Hughes was no ordinary attendee, however: she arrived at the ceremony as a history-making performer, the youngest ever to earn a nomination for best actress.

An ordinary childhood

Castle-Hughes was born on March 24, 1990, in Donnybrook, Western Australia. Her father, Tim Castle, is Australian, while her mother, Desrae Hughes, is a Maori from New Zealand. The Maori, a people of Polynesian descent, were the first to populate New Zealand, possibly as long ago as 800 C.E. When Castle-Hughes was four years old, she and her family moved to New Zealand, a nation consisting primarily of two large islands, the North Island and the South Island. She now lives on the North Island in Glenn Innes, near Auckland, New Zealand's largest city. Castle-Hughes has two younger brothers, Rhys and Liam.

> "A long time ago, my ancestor Paikea came to this place on the back of a whale. Since then, in every generation of my family, the first-born son has carried his name and become the leader of our tribe … until now."
>
> **Keisha Castle-Hughes, as Paikea, in *Whale Rider***

Prior to being cast in *Whale Rider,* Castle-Hughes had experienced a typical childhood, attending school, arguing with her brothers over whose turn it was to wash the dishes, and spending time with friends. She told Eleanor Black of the *New Zealand Herald,* "I'm always on the phone. When I'm not with a friend, I'm on the phone to a friend and when I'm not on the phone to a friend, I'm on the net to a friend, so I'm always with friends." She had wanted to become an actress one day, although she had been warned this was a difficult path. Upon expressing her theatrical ambitions during a career fair at her school, she was advised to seek a more "realistic" profession. According to an article in *Entertainment Weekly,* she recalled, "I always said I wanted to be an actor and people were like, 'It's not going to happen. It's a great dream, but let's get real here.'"

Whale Rider: The Novel

The screenplay for the movie *Whale Rider,* adapted for film by director Niki Caro, was based on a novel by Witi Ihimaera. Born in Gisborne, New Zealand, in 1944, Ihimaera has been credited with writing the first Maori novel—*Tangi,* released in 1973. Best known for his works written for adults, Ihimaera has also published books for a younger audience, including his young-adult novel *Whale Rider.* The film's success brought the author, already celebrated in his native land, significant exposure worldwide.

Like the film, the novel focuses on a young girl, though her name in the book is Kahu rather than Pai. The chapters alternate between narration of the girl's story by her uncle, Rawiri, and an account of the legendary whale rider, founder of the Maori people. As with her film counterpart, Kahu displays the qualities of a natural leader, but she meets with anger and resistance on the part of her great-grandfather, who cannot accept the idea of a female tribal chief. Supported and loved by her less-traditional great-grandmother, Nanny Flowers, Kahu develops the confidence to challenge her tribe's ancient conventions. (In the film these characters are the girl's grandparents rather than great-grandparents.) In a review of the novel in *Booklist,* Gillian Engberg described it as a challenging work because of its multiple story lines and difficult subject matter, but asserted that the book is well worth the effort: "[Ihimaera] combines breathtaking, poetic imagery, hilarious family dialogue, and scenes that beautifully juxtapose contemporary and ancient culture."

An extraordinary adolescence

When director Niki Caro and casting director Diana Rowan visited her school in Mt. Wellington in 2001, Castle-Hughes had no way of knowing the impact that visit would have on her life. Nearly ten years earlier, Rowan had discovered Anna Paquin, also a Kiwi, or New Zealander, and cast her in the Oscar-winning film *The Piano.* Paquin won an Academy Award for best supporting actress in that film and has gone on to star in several successful films, including the *X-Men* series. Just as she had done with Paquin, Rowan detected untapped acting potential in Castle-Hughes, and the eleven-year-old was chosen to star as Paikea in Caro's upcoming film *Whale Rider.* In her biography on the official Web site for *Whale Rider,* Castle-Hughes recalled her reaction when she learned she had gotten the role of Pai: "I was just speechless, I didn't know what to say. About two hours later I was running around the hotel just screaming. I was so overwhelmed!"

Castle-Hughes spent about two months filming *Whale Rider* in Whangara, a small seaside village on the eastern coast of New Zealand. With the help of her tutor, Stephanie Wilkin, and director Caro, Castle-

Hughes received a crash course in acting, learning the basics of her craft and getting to know the character she would play. Castle-Hughes recalled at the film's Web site: "Stef and Niki showed me how to find my feelings and how to talk properly. Then after a couple of weeks I just fell into the character. I didn't need to look back on anything because I could feel the character so much." She earned praise from the filmmakers and her fellow actors for her dedication, her professionalism, and her ability to portray complex emotions in a believable way.

Whale Rider

Based on a book by Maori author Witi Ihimaera, *Whale Rider* depicts a crisis in the world of a Maori tribe known as Ngati Kanohi. The tribal elders struggle to make their ancient traditions relevant to the young people in the tribe, many of whom feel a strong attraction to the values and popular culture of Western society. The leader of the tribe, Koro, finds himself in a difficult position: tribal tradition dictates that the leader be a first-born male descendant of the legendary Paikea, who arrived at the shores of New Zealand one thousand years ago on the back of a whale. But a tragedy in Koro's family has undermined that tradition: while in labor delivering her twin daughter and son, Koro's daughter-in-law dies, as does the baby boy. The grief-stricken father, Koro's son Porourangi, names his daughter Paikea, breaking with tradition by giving a girl the name of the male tribal ancestor. Koro, desperately worried about the tribe's future now that the male heir has died, urges his son to quickly remarry and produce a male heir. Pourarangi responds by fleeing New Zealand, leaving his daughter to be raised by her grandparents.

That little girl, nicknamed Pai, grows up in the shadow of her grandfather's disappointment that his one surviving grandchild is a girl. To Koro it is unthinkable that a girl could take on the responsibility of leading the tribe. He begins conducting training sessions for local boys, teaching them the tribe's ancient warrior ways in the hope of finding a natural leader among them. Pai watches the proceedings secretly, wanting to participate in the classes but forbidden by her grandfather from taking part. Despite his orders, Pai practices on the sly, mastering the warrior arts and learning about other aspects of her tribe's customs. She is deeply hurt by her grandfather's rejection but

Actress Sigourney Weaver and Academy president Frank Pierson announce the nominees for the 2004 best leading actress Oscar. Pictured on the screen behind them, from lower left: Keisha Castle-Hughes, Diane Keaton, Samantha Morton, Charlize Theron, and Naomi Watts. AP/Wide World Photos. Reproduced by permission.

somehow remains steadfast in her belief that she is destined to lead her tribe and that her grandfather will eventually recognize that fact.

When several whales are stranded on Whangara's beach, many in the community interpret the situation as a dire warning for the tribe itself. They consider the whales sacred, and if the beached whales die, it would seem to forecast more trouble for the Ngati Kanohi people. The entire town bands together in an effort to get the whales back into the water, but their efforts are unsuccessful. In an extraordinary display of courage and leadership, Pai goes to the beach alone, climbs on the back of one of the whales and, like her legendary namesake, rides the whale through the ocean water.

The aftermath

Whale Rider, a small movie from the distant country of New Zealand that starred native actors as well as non-actors who had never before been in a film, achieved a surprising level of success in the United States, Europe, and elsewhere. The film earned more than $40 million at box offices worldwide, a respectable sum for any movie and a shocking amount for a film made well outside the Hollywood mainstream, with a budget of about $4 million. *Whale Rider* won audience awards at such important festivals as the Toronto Film Festival in Ontario, Canada, and the Sundance Film Festival in the United States. At the New Zealand film awards the film won honors for best film, writer, and director, with Castle-Hughes taking home the trophy for best actress.

Of her many awards and accomplishments, Castle-Hughes's Academy Award nomination for best actress earned her the most attention worldwide. The youngest-ever nominee lost to Charlize Theron, star of *Monster,* but for thirteen-year-old Castle-Hughes, being in Los Angeles, appearing on the *Tonight Show with Jay Leno* and the *Oprah Winfrey Show,* and attending the Oscar ceremonies provided sufficient excitement to overcome any disappointment. While she enjoyed the hoopla surrounding the Academy Awards, Castle-Hughes, viewing the Hollywood scene for the first time, expressed a hint of skepticism in a February of 2004 article in the *New Zealand Herald:* "Here it's all based on these awards and these awards and these awards, and if your life doesn't revolve around it, then what are you doing in Los Angeles?" She also expressed amusement regarding the numerous gift baskets she received as an Academy Award nominee: "What am I going to do with acid peel and wrinkle remover? And you get all these gift certificates for places in Beverly Hills—I'm like, I live twelve hours away from here."

Following her whirlwind tour of the American entertainment industry, Castle-Hughes eagerly returned home to her friends and family, hoping to get back to her normal life but unsure whether that would be possible. In early 2003, just as her fame was spreading from the success of *Whale Rider,* Castle-Hughes told the *New Zealand Herald* of her anxieties about enrolling at a new school: "I think it would be nice if I could meet people as me, but that's not going to be possible. I'm going to meet people as 'the whale rider' and it's going to be hard, even as fun as it's going to be. I want to meet people on my own steam." Coping with newfound fame and the changes it brings will continue to be a factor in Castle-Hughes's life; she plays the Queen of Naboo in the upcoming film *Star Wars: Episode III,* due in 2005.

For More Information

Periodicals

Baillie, Russell. "Keisha's Big Worry, Heels and Red Carpet." *New Zealand Herald* (February 28, 2004).

Bal, Sumeet. "Keisha Castle-Hughes: *Whale Rider*." *Entertainment Weekly* (February 6, 2004): p. 50.

Black, Eleanor. "Taking *Rider* in Her Stride." *New Zealand Herald* (January 25, 2003).

Engberg, Gillian. "*The Whale Rider.*" *Booklist* (July 2003): p. 1881.

Linden, Sheri. "*Whale Rider.*" *Hollywood Reporter* (June 6, 2003): p. 25.

Sorensen, Marlene. "New Zealand Girl Power." *Time International* (August 11, 2003): p. 58.

Web sites

"Keisha Castle-Hughes: Pai." *Whale Rider: The Movie.* http://www.whale riderthemovie.com/html/castcrew_cast.html (accessed on April 29, 2004).

Coldplay

Rock group

From the time of British-bred sensation Coldplay's first major-label release in the summer of 2000, music journalists have written that the band doesn't quite fit in with the current popular-music landscape. Their soulful, haunting, intelligent songs have set them apart from bubblegum pop stars, aggressive rap artists, and what Tom Sinclair of *Entertainment Weekly* described as "the hordes of thuggish, blustering nu-metal bands or Identikit junior-league punk outfits." Much has been made in Britain's music press of lead singer Chris Martin's clean-living ways and general distaste for alcohol—a far cry from the lifestyle of a stereotypical rock star. The band has shied away from corporate endorsements, choosing to promote causes that address world poverty or environmental issues rather than lending their music to commercials selling cars or sneakers or computer software. In spite of—or perhaps because of—the ways in which they differ from their peers, Coldplay has become a sensation, selling millions of records, earning numerous major awards, and garnering praise from music critics all over the

From left, John Buckland, Chris Martin, Will Champion, and Guy Berryman of Coldplay. © S.I.N./ Corbis.

world. In an article in *Maclean's* magazine, Coldplay guitarist Jon Buckland explained that connecting to listeners on an emotional level "is the most important thing in music for us. We're not really the cool, detached kind of people; we're really passionate about what we're doing." At Coldplay's official Web site, Martin further explained the band's reason for being: "We were trying to say that there is an alternative. That you can try to be catchy without being slick, poppy without being pop, and you can be uplifting without being pompous.... We wanted to be a reaction against soulless rubbish."

The birth of a sensation

The members of Coldplay met and became friends while living in the same dormitory at the University College of London (UCL) in the mid-

1990s. They formed a band, originally naming themselves Starfish. When friends of theirs who were playing in a band called Coldplay no longer wanted to use the name, Starfish officially became Coldplay. The name was taken from a book of poetry called *Child's Reflections, Cold Play*. The group comprises bassist Guy Berryman, guitarist Buckland, drummer Will Champion, and lead singer, guitarist, and pianist Martin. Martin had wanted to be a musician since the age of eleven. He explained to Katherine Turman of *Mother Jones* that when he began attending UCL, he was more interested in finding bandmates than in studying his major, ancient history. Asked by Turman whether he started his education thinking he would become an ancient history teacher,

> ## "Our sound will change, but all we care about is melody and emotion."
>
> **Chris Martin, Coldplay e-zine, www.coldplay.com, November 2003.**

Martin jokingly responded, "That was my real dream, but then Coldplay came about!" Three of the four members did complete their university education (Berryman dropped out partway through), with much of their free time spent writing music and rehearsing.

In April of 1998 Coldplay went into the recording studio with the intention of recording a demo CD to use as a calling card for introducing the band to record labels. The recording session went so well that the band decided to release the three songs as an EP—a recording of a few songs, shorter in duration than a regular full-length album—that was titled *Safety*. They made five hundred copies, most of which were given to radio stations, newspapers, music magazines, family members, and friends. In the audience at one of Coldplay's live shows in a London club was Simon Williams, a music journalist and the founder of independent record label Fierce Panda. Williams was so impressed by the band that he signed them to his label. With the label's financial backing, Coldplay returned to the studio in February of 1999 to record the EP *Brothers and Sisters*. With this release, Coldplay began earning the attention of England's music reviewers and radio hosts. In 1999 the influential British magazine *New Musical*

Making a Difference

While many of Coldplay's songs concern personal subjects like love, heartbreak, and insecurity, Martin and the rest of the band have also focused on global issues, particularly speaking out for fair trade as part of Oxfam's Make Trade Fair campaign (www.maketradefair.com). Oxfam is a collection of non-governmental organizations working all over the world to reduce poverty and improve lives.

During 2002 Oxfam invited Coldplay to tour Haiti and see firsthand the problems experienced by farmers in a developing nation, and to learn about the impact the World Trade Organization (WTO) has had on these farmers. In an interview with *Mother Jones,* Martin confessed that he and the other members of Coldplay knew almost nothing about world trade issues before their visit to Haiti: "We hadn't any idea about it. But you go on a trip and learn how the importing and exporting of goods around the world works, and you realize it's a huge crisis." Appalled by the dire poverty in Haiti and convinced that social activism, particularly when practiced by a world-famous band, could make a difference, Coldplay began discussing world trade and promoting Make Trade Fair whenever possible. The band members have explained to anyone who will listen that WTO rules allow inexpensive American and European crops, grown by farmers who receive financial help from their governments, to flood the markets in poor nations, making it much harder for farmers in places like Haiti and Mexico to sell their own crops.

The members of Coldplay have also supported environmental causes. At their Web site, Coldplay has asked fans who wish to write them letters to send e-mails, in part because such transmissions are "easier on the environment" than traditional paper letters. In addition, the band has joined with a United Kingdom company called Future Forests to plant ten thousand mango trees in India. As explained on the Future Forests Web site, "the trees provide fruit for trade and local consumption and over their lifetime will soak up the carbon dioxide emitted by the production and distribution of Coldplay's best-selling album *A Rush of Blood to the Head.*" Numerous environmental experts believe that harmful carbon dioxide emissions coming from sources such as factories, cars, and furnaces have begun to change Earth's climate and, if not curbed, will lead to devastating consequences produced by global warming.

At the band's Web site, bassist Guy Berryman explained why he and his bandmates feel compelled to promote these causes: "Anyone in our position has a certain responsibility. Odd though it may seem to us, a lot of people … read what we're saying, see us on TV, buy our records and read the sleeves, and that can be a great platform. You can make people aware of issues. It isn't very much effort for us at all, but if it can help people, then we want to do it."

Express (*NME*) labeled Coldplay the new band to watch, and Steve Lamacq of the British Broadcasting Corporation (BBC) Radio 1 gave Coldplay's music plenty of airtime, helping the song "Brothers and Sisters" enter Britain's pop music charts at number ninety-two.

Brothers and Sisters made an impression not only on radio listeners and music critics but also on Dan Keeling of Parlophone

Records. Keeling signed Coldplay to the label in 1999, and the band went into the studio to record their first major-label effort. This EP, *The Blue Room*, was released in the autumn of 1999. Thanks to an intense touring schedule, continued support from Radio 1, and the band's ongoing polishing of their musical skills, Coldplay's fan base widened. Parlophone felt the band was ready for a higher profile, and the group began to record their first full-length CD, *Parachutes.*

Coldplay gets hot

In March of 2000 Coldplay released "Shiver," the first single from *Parachutes.* "Shiver" made a splash, reaching number thirty-five on England's music charts, but it was the second single from *Parachutes* that catapulted Coldplay to stardom. "Yellow," released in June of 2000, became a genuine hit in both England and the United States, where it came to the attention of the public as a video on MTV and then went into heavy rotation at radio stations all across the country. Thrilled with their newfound international success, the band nonetheless worried about overexposure. During their 2001 visit to Live 105, an alternative rock radio station in San Francisco, a station employee showed Buckland the station's current playlist, with "Yellow" in the number-one spot. In the week prior, the station had played "Yellow" fifty-one times. Buckland remarked to *Entertainment Weekly* in March of 2001, "It's cool. But fifty-one times? That's, like, seven times a day. Even I'd get sick of it."

Far from getting sick of Coldplay's music, however, critics and fans celebrated the arrival of a band with a seemingly endless supply of soaring melodies, emotional outpourings, and pensive but ultimately upbeat lyrics. *Parachutes* was nominated for the prestigious Mercury Music Prize in 2000, and in 2001 the album earned two BRIT Awards (similar to the Grammy Awards in the United States) for best British group and best British album. The following year *Parachutes* won the Grammy Award for best alternative music album. In the band's biography on the Coldplay Web site, Champion explained that their success has been "all on our own terms. We have 100 percent control over any aspect of whatever we do, and that's really important to who we are and the music we make." All band members share in the songwriting credits, co-produce their recordings, and oversee production of their videos and the selection of artwork for their CDs. Even the photograph on the cover of *Parachutes,* of a spinning globe lit from within, is credited to Coldplay.

Following the album's release in the summer of 2000, Coldplay hit the road, touring the United Kingdom, Europe, and the United States. The tour proved exhausting, with the 2001 U.S. tour plagued by bad weather and illness among band members. Several cancelled shows inspired rumors that the band was on the verge of a breakup, but such gossip was unfounded. By the end of the tour, Coldplay's members were in dire need of a long rest, but they had accomplished their mission: they had brought their music to the masses, and the masses were happily singing along.

What a *Rush*

Emotionally and physically drained from the long months of touring, Coldplay returned home for a respite before beginning work on their second album. Amid speculation that their second album could not meet the expectations generated by the first, band members made statements to the press that they would rather release no album at all than release a substandard recording. According to the Coldplay Web site, after a few months of recording, "Everyone was happy—except the band." Buckland recalled in the band's online biography: "We were pleased with it, but then we took a step back and realised that it wasn't right. It would have been easy to say we'd done enough, to release an album to keep up the momentum, but we didn't." They went back to a small studio in Liverpool where much of *Parachutes* had been recorded, and took another stab at it. This time, they found exactly what they were looking for. "Songs like 'Daylight,' 'The Whisper,' and 'The Scientist' splurged out over two weeks, and we recorded them very quickly," Martin remembered. "We just felt completely inspired, and felt we could do anything we liked."

The extra effort paid off, and *A Rush of Blood to the Head* was released in the summer of 2002 to a chorus of positive reviews. *Hollywood Reporter* summed up the feelings of many: "It's an even better album than the first, a superb collection of sonically and lyrically adventurous songs that have the kind of hooks that burrow into your brain on a first hearing and a depth that resonates long afterward."

Coldplay earned a slew of awards for their sophomore album, including three MTV Video Music Awards in 2003, a Grammy Award for best alternative music album in 2003 and, for the song "Clocks," a Grammy for record of the year in 2004. The band also won, once again, the BRIT Awards for best British group and best British album.

Mary Kaye Schilling wrote in *Entertainment Weekly* about the nearly constant radio play of *A Rush of Blood to the Head,* and described it as being "stalked by Coldplay—in restaurants, yoga class, even the toilet at the gas station, for crying out loud." Even in the midst of international success and abundant media coverage, however, Coldplay managed to keep a relatively low profile, and band members could still go about their daily lives without worrying about being recognized and swarmed by fans. Their anonymity was threatened, however, when frontman Martin began dating American actress Gwyneth Paltrow (1973–) in the summer of 2002, bringing the singer a new level of celebrity. In December of 2003, the couple announced Pal-

Coldplay accepts their 2004 Record of the Year Grammy. AP/Wide World Photos. Reproduced by permission.

trow's pregnancy and, soon after, their marriage. Their daughter, Apple Blythe Alison Martin, was born in May of 2004.

After another intense round of touring to support the release of *A Rush of Blood to the Head,* Coldplay attempted to take a break from the spotlight, returning to England and the recording studio to create their third album. In the meantime they released *Live 2003,* a CD and DVD package chronicling a concert performed in Sydney, Australia, with the DVD featuring additional behind-the-scenes coverage of the tour. MacKenzie Wilson of the *All Music Guide* Web site described the release as "a resilient, bright package of glorious rock & roll."

For More Information

Periodicals

Browne, David. "Uncommon Coldplay." *Entertainment Weekly* (March 16, 2001): p. 32.

Deziel, Shanda. "Music: Hot and Cold." *Maclean's* (October 7, 2002): p. 62.

Diehl, Matt. "Matt Diehl Talks to the Rest of the Band." *Interview* (August 2003): p. 119.

Scheck, Frank. "Coldplay." *Hollywood Reporter* (August 14, 2002): p. 12.

Schilling, Mary Kaye. "Coldplay: The New Romantics." *Entertainment Weekly* (December 26, 2003): p. 36.

Sinclair, Tom. "Even Better Cold." *Entertainment Weekly* (October 25, 2002): p. L2T5.

Turman, Katherine. "Chris Martin: Fair Trade's Charm Offensive." *Mother Jones* (January-February 2004): p. 78.

Web sites

Coldplay Official Web site. http://www.coldplay.com (accessed on May 7, 2004).

"Coldplay: Bio." *MTV.com.* http://www.mtv.com/bands/az/coldplay/bio.jhtml (accessed on May 3, 2004).

"Coldplay's Forest: Tree Tubes." *Future Forests.* http://www.futureforests.com/acatalog/Future_Forests_Coldplay_s_Forest__Tree_Tubes_151.html (accessed on May 7, 2004).

Wilson, MacKenzie. "Coldplay." *All Music Guide.* http://www.allmusic.com (accessed on May 7, 2004).

Sofia Coppola

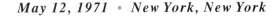

May 12, 1971 • *New York, New York*

Director, screenwriter, producer, designer, photographer

Sofia Coppola was born into Hollywood royalty, the daughter of one of the most applauded film directors of the twentieth century, Francis Ford Coppola (1939–). From the beginning, it seemed she was destined, like her father, for a career in the movies. A few weeks after her birth, Coppola took on her first acting role: as an infant boy in her father's epic film, *The Godfather* (1972). Throughout her life, she continued to live and work under her father's wing, but his wing often cast a long shadow. In 2004 Coppola finally stepped out of that shadow to claim her own celebrity. She became the first American woman to be nominated for an Academy Award for Best Director, for her movie *Lost in Translation* (2003).

An artistic household

Sofia Coppola was born May 12, 1971, in New York City, during the production of *The Godfather.* She was the youngest child, and the only daughter, of director, producer, screenwriter Francis Ford Coppola and Eleanor Coppola, a designer, artist, and documentary filmmaker. Sofia, and her older brothers, Roman and Gian Carlo, grew up on the sets of their father's movies, with their mother close at hand, often documenting the movie-making process.

The youngest Coppola loved traveling to such exotic film locations as Manila, located in the Philippines, where the filming of *Apocalypse Now* (1979) took place. *Apocalypse Now* is Francis Ford Coppola's powerful look at the Vietnam War (1954–75). Seven-year-old Sofia entertained herself for hours by drawing elaborate pictures of palm trees and helicopters and weaving the pictures together to form a story.

> **"I felt a little bit this time, a little bit, like people were able to see my movie without seeing my family."**

When not on location the family settled in a small town in Napa Valley, California, away from the glare of Hollywood. Even at home, however, family life was far from ordinary. The Coppolas had summer creativity camps, where the children were encouraged to write stories and plays, to design and experiment. Sofia's parents inspired her, but Eleanor Coppola has also noted that her daughter was a very imaginative child from the beginning. According to a now-famous story, Francis Ford Coppola claims that he knew his daughter was destined to be a director when she was about three years old. As Coppola has told it, he and wife were driving in their car, bickering back and forth and not paying attention to Sofia, who was sitting in the backseat. Tired of her parents arguing, Sofia called out, "Cut!"

The acting bug bites back

Coppola not only visited her father's movie locations, she also had small roles in his films, including *Rumblefish* and *The Outsiders,* both

The Family Business

Under the circumstances it is not surprising that Sofia Coppola went into the family business; her family tree reads like a who's who of Hollywood. Grandfather Carmine Coppola (1910–1991) was a flutist, conductor, and composer who worked with a number of symphonies across the United States. He found fame in his later years when he migrated to Hollywood and wrote music for the movies, especially those directed or produced by his son, Francis Ford Coppola. In 1974, he won an Oscar for writing the score for Francis Ford's *The Godfather, Part II.*

Sofia's aunt is actress Talia Shire (1946–), the sister of Francis Ford. Shire is probably best known for her role as Adrian in *Rocky* (1976), for which she received an Academy Award nomination for Best Actress. Shire's son is actor Jason Schwartzman (1980–), who starred in *Rushmore* (1998). Sofia's more famous cousin is actor Nicolas Cage (1964–),

son of August Coppola, Francis Ford's brother. Cage won the Best Actor Oscar for his performance in *Leaving Las Vegas* (1995).

Sofia's brother, Roman Coppola (1965–), is also in film and was a familiar face on the set of *The Virgin Suicides* and *Lost in Translation.* He served as his sister's assistant director on both movies.

Sofia Coppola even married a filmmaker, director Spike Jonze (1969–), whom she met while a student at the California Institute of the Arts (CalArts). Some claimed that the character of the flashy photographer husband in *Lost in Translation* was based on Jonze and that Coppola wrote the story because she was having trouble in her marriage. Coppola denied the rumors, although she admits that most of what she writes comes from her personal experiences. In 2003 Coppola and Jonze separated after four years of marriage.

released in 1983 and both based on the popular novels of author S. E. Hinton (1948–), who writes books for children and young adults. Coppola also appeared in *The Cotton Club* (1984) and *Peggy Sue Got Married* (1986). Her biggest role, however, came in 1990 when her father tapped her to play Mary Corleone in *The Godfather, Part III.*

When the movie was released, critics had a field day. Reviewers openly criticized Francis Ford Coppola for showing favoritism and casting his own daughter in such an important role. His daughter, however, was never his first choice. Actress Winona Ryder (1971–) was originally cast, but backed out at the last minute because of illness. As a favor to her father, Sofia agreed to take the part. This was a big step for her because, although she had been in several movies, she was extremely camera shy. "I never wanted to be an actor," Coppola told Karen Valby in *Entertainment Weekly.* "It's not my personality." Coppola was not rewarded for her bravery. Instead, critics raked her over the coals, poking fun at her accent and claiming that she gave a horribly wooden performance.

Coppola was so upset by the harsh criticism that she gave up acting, appearing in only a few more films, including *Star Wars: Episode I The Phantom Menace* (1999). The camera-shy young woman, however, had other interests.

What's a girl to do?

While still in high school Coppola was already dabbling in fashion and design. She modeled for American designer Marc Jacobs (1964–) and interned at Chanel, a famous fashion house in Paris, France. As an intern, she mostly answered phones, made photocopies, and ran errands, but the experience, says Coppola, was remarkable.

After graduating from Napa Valley's St. Helena High School, Coppola briefly attended college in Oakland, California. She then enrolled at California Institute of the Arts (CalArts) in Valencia, California, where she studied painting for several years before dropping out. By now, Coppola was in her early twenties. She toyed with the idea of going to film school in New York, but school did not seem to be the place for her. Instead, she began to explore different career options. For a while she worked as a photographer, taking pictures for such fashion magazines as *Paris Vogue* and *Allure*.

Eventually Coppola turned to fashion design when she and a longtime friend started a sportswear clothing label called Milk Fed. Coppola focused on design while her friend took charge of production. Over the years the venture grew, and eventually became quite successful. The current line consists mostly of logo imprinted T-shirts and clothing inspired by 1980s fashion. Coppola also launched her own boutique, Heaven-27, to sell the hip Milk Fed line. Stores are based in Los Angeles and Japan, where Heaven-27 is considered one of the coolest stores in the country.

Coppola worried that she was going in too many directions, and that maybe she should focus her energies. Coppola went to her father for advice, asking him if she should settle with one thing and specialize. The senior Coppola recalled telling his daughter "that she didn't have to, that she should pursue everything and anything that interested her, that eventually they'd come together in something on their own."

Everything comes together

Coppola tried her hand at painting, photography, fashion design, acting, and even hosting a show on television. In 1995 she and Zoe Cassavetes, daughter of director John Cassavetes (1929–1989), appeared on *Hi-Octane,* a weekly show on Comedy Central that was geared toward teens and focused on movies, fashion, and celebrities. The program was short-lived.

In 1998, however, everything finally seemed to come together. That was the year that Coppola wrote, directed, and produced her first film, a short comedy called *Lick the Star.* It was not the first time that she had tried her hand behind the camera. In 1989 she helped her father write the script for a short film titled *Life without Zoe,* which was part of the anthology movie *New York Stories*. She also designed the costumes for the movie. *Lick the Star,* however, was Coppola's first attempt at taking creative control of a film project, and, after making the movie, she declared that she had figured out what she wanted to do.

Coppola lost no time in pursuing her dream. In 1999, only one year later, she released her first feature-length film, *The Virgin Suicides*. Coppola wrote the screenplay, which was adapted from the 1993 book by American author Jeffrey Eugenides (1960–). The movie was produced by Zoetrope, her father's film company. This time, although some critics focused on the fact that a Hollywood kid was being given a boost by her famous father, most were not as harsh as they had been in 1990 when Coppola appeared in *The Godfather, Part III*. In fact, the majority of reviewers embraced the very bizarre story of a group of teenage boys in a suburb of Detroit, Michigan, obsessed with five sisters who, by the movie's end, kill themselves.

Many of Coppola's skills helped her to make *The Virgin Suicides* a success, especially her photographer's eye and her flair for design. Since the story is told from the perspective of several different boys, she used a lot of quick camera shots as if the boys were taking snapshots. And, because the story is set in the 1970s, she wanted to get the right feel in the look of the film and in the clothes the actors wore. Coppola was viewed as a young, new director who had a lot of potential, and critics looked forward to her next film.

A story all her own

The success of *The Virgin Suicides* led Coppola to try her hand at writing an original screenplay. She had been thinking about a story for several years, one that would take place in Tokyo, Japan, where she had spent a lot of time working on her clothing line and shooting ads for fashion magazines. The outcome was *Lost in Translation* (2003), which Coppola not only wrote, but produced and directed.

The movie is a look at two unhappy Americans who cross paths in Tokyo. One is a middle-aged celebrity named Bob Harris, played by Bill Murray (1950–), who is alone in Japan to shoot a whiskey commercial. The other is Charlotte, a young girl just out of college, whose photographer husband leaves her behind as he goes off on extended photo assignments. Coppola explores how the two cope with the unfamiliar neon culture of Japan. Bob and Charlotte are also two people, at different points in their lives, who are unsure of who they are and what their places are in the world. According to Coppola, who spoke with *Entertainment Weekly* in October 2003, that is how she felt when she was younger: "I just remember feeling overwhelmed by 'How do you figure out what you're supposed to do?'"

Coppola shot the movie on location in Tokyo in just twenty-seven days, for only $4 million, which in movie-making, is a very small budget. There is no fast action, no special effects, just a simple story about two people who connect. As she did in *The Virgin Suicides,* Coppola drew on her background in design and photography to create her own personal style of filmmaking. Her cast and crew noticed. Her critics noticed. According to David Ansen, in *Newsweek,* "Coppola is a warm, meticulous observer, with an intimate style that's the polar opposite of her famous father, Francis Ford. He's grand opera. This is chamber music."

Coppola makes history

Critics heaped additional praise on *Lost in Translation,* describing it as elegant and lyrical. Some even called it flawless. With the praise came the awards. The movie took home three Golden Globes: Best Picture and Best Director for Coppola, and Best Actor for Murray. The Golden Globes are awarded each year by members of the Hollywood Foreign

Press Association for outstanding achievement in film and television. Coppola also received top honors from the New York Film Critics Circle and at the Independent Spirit Awards, which honor smaller films that are not made by huge Hollywood studios.

In 2004, however, the thirty-two-year-old filmmaker made history. She became the first American woman to be nominated as Best Director by the Academy of Motion Picture Arts and Sciences. Each year the academy, composed of members of the film community, gives awards, known as Oscars, to individuals who excel in such areas as screenwriting, acting, editing, and directing. Coppola followed in the footsteps of only two women: Italian director Lina Wertmuller (1928–), nominated in 1976 for *Seven Beauties,* and New Zealand-born director Jane Campion (1954–), nominated in 1993 for *The Piano.*

Coppola won the 2004 Oscar for Best Original Screenplay, but she lost the award for Best Director to Peter Jackson (1961–), director of *The Lord of the Rings: The Return of the King.* Her place in history, however, and her reputation as a respected filmmaker was set. All the years of dabbling and searching, observing and experimenting, had finally paid off.

Sophia Coppola poses with her Academy Award for Original Screenplay for Lost in Translation. AP/Wide World Photos. Reproduced by permission.

Interviewers describe Sofia Coppola's films as dreamy or dreamlike. They use the same words to describe Coppola the filmmaker. Still a shy, quiet person, Coppola seems uncomfortable in the spotlight of her new-found fame. According to Anthony Breznican, who interviewed her in 2004, she is "polite, pensive and as unpolished" as the character of Charlotte in *Lost in Translation.* She is also eager to move on to her next film, which is expected to be about the life of Marie Antoinette (1755–1793), the notorious eighteenth-century queen of France.

For More Information

Periodicals

Ansen, David. "Scarlett Fever." *Newsweek* (September 15, 2003): p. 64.

Betts, Kate. "Sofia's Choice." *Time* (September 15, 2003): p. 70.

Corliss, Richard. "Sundance Sorority." *Time* (January 24, 2000): pp. 68–69.

Gehring, Wes. D. "Along Comes Another Coppola." *USA Today* (January 2004): p. 59.

Krueger, Lisa. "Sofia Coppola." *Interview* (April 2000): p. 46.

Valby, Karen. "Fresh Heir: By Following in Her Father's Footsteps, a Young Filmmaker Finds Her Own Way." *Entertainment Weekly* (October 3, 2003): p. 51.

Valby, Karen. "Sofia Coppola: Lost in Translation." *Entertainment Weekly* (February 6, 2004): p. 94.

Paige Davis

October 15, 1969 • *Philadelphia, Pennsylvania*

Television host

U·X·L newsmakers • volume 1

When Paige Davis signed on in 2001 as the host of *Trading Spaces*, a home-improvement show on cable television's The Learning Channel (TLC), she thought of it as a way to learn about performing on television without actually being in the spotlight. She explained to Charlie Huisking of the *Sarasota Herald Tribune*, "When I auditioned, I had no idea what it would become. I figured it would be a chance to spread my wings and cut my chops on TV, hidden away on cable on a show no one would see. Boy, was I wrong." After Davis joined the show, the number of viewers steadily increased, with millions tuning in to each episode. Soon *Trading Spaces* became one of the most popular shows on regular cable, the network increased the number of shows each season from forty-five to sixty, and Davis had become a star. She has appeared on such national television programs as the *Tonight Show with Jay Leno* and the *Today Show,* and her image has appeared twice on the cover of *TV Guide*. She also earned high-

profile roles in stage productions, including the part of Roxie Hart in the Broadway production of *Chicago*.

A natural performer

Born in 1969 in Philadelphia, Pennsylvania, Mindy Paige Davis spent many of her childhood years in Prairie Sun, Wisconsin. When she was thirteen years old, she came across her mother's copy of the *West Side Story* cast recording. Listening to the music from this celebrated Broadway show, Davis fell in love with the songs and with the idea of becoming a performer. She memorized the words to every song and

> "Even if we got canceled right now, I really believe that *Trading Spaces* completely affected a genre of television, and it made its mark. Everybody's copying us because they want their own show that people adore and are committed to. Our fans are so loyal."

spent hours acting out the show, playing various parts. She knew she wanted to dance and sing, not just in her own living room but on stage in front of an audience. In an interview with Kate Coyne in *Good Housekeeping*, Davis related, "Dancing is my life.... I didn't start dancing until I was fourteen, but I knew immediately that it was what I wanted to do for the rest of my life." Davis's family moved to Louisville, Kentucky, where she attended high school at the Youth Performing Arts School. After high school graduation Davis attended the Meadows School of the Arts at Southern Methodist University in Dallas, Texas. She honed her performing skills working in summer stock and regional theater, and soon after graduating from college, Davis moved to Los Angeles to look for work as a performer.

Home Improvement Around the Clock

The hugely popular *Trading Spaces* is just one among many home renovation programs populating the cable landscape, each with its own twist. Some, like the long-running *This Old House* (PBS), focus exclusively on home renovation, demonstrating techniques and giving practical advice for viewers. Others combine elements of traditional home improvement shows with fly-on-the-wall reality television, throwing in a race against time or a high-stakes competition among friends.

Trading Spaces itself has generated two spin-offs: *Trading Spaces: Family* and *Trading Spaces: Home Free.* In the family edition, kids participate in the neighborly redesign efforts. *Home Free* is a home redesign tournament with multiple neighbors competing against one another to win the ultimate homeowner prize: a paid-off mortgage.

On *While You Were Out* (TLC), one member of a household is lured away for two days while a designer and crew of workers redesign a room or revamp the yard. Intensity builds as the crew races to complete the project before the absent person returns home for the big surprise. *Weekend Warriors* (HGTV) features homeowners spending a weekend on a home-improvement project. This show lacks the element of surprise so crucial to *Trading Spaces* and *While You Were Out,* but it allows viewers to see the emotional and physical strain placed on the homeowners who have to complete their own project without the help of designers or professional carpenters.

Monster House (Discovery) is a home-renovation show on steroids. While the homeowners camp out in an RV in front of their home, a work crew spends five days drastically redesigning several rooms in their house. The projects usually conform to a theme, including Old West House, Race Car House, and Amusement Park House. Not only do the residents receive a brand-new look for their home, the workers also earn a deluxe tool package if they finish the project on time. On a smaller scale, *In a Fix* (TLC) rescues do-it-yourself homeowners who begin a project only to find themselves in the midst of a disastrous project. Called in by a member of the family, the show's crew arrives to fix the problem and toss in a redesign of the room while they're at it.

In Los Angeles Davis won roles in commercials and videos and even toured with the Beach Boys as a dancer. While she found steady work in the entertainment industry for several years, she was unable to secure a breakthrough role that would make her a top-tier performer. In 1997 she finally got a major role, playing Babette the feather duster in the national touring company of the stage show *Beauty and the Beast*. She spent two and one-half years touring as Babette, gaining experience that could launch her career on the stage. Lumière, the character in the show who pursues Babette, was played by actor Patrick Page, who became Davis's real-life love interest and, eventually, her husband. (Many observers have noted that, had Davis not kept her maiden name after getting married, she would be known as

Paige Page.) Davis's experience in the cast of *Beauty and the Beast* led to her next role, dancing in the Broadway musical *Chicago*. In the Las Vegas production of the show Davis served as the understudy to Chita Rivera for the lead role of Roxie Hart.

Trading up to TV

In 2001 Davis put her promising musical theater career on hold to pursue an entirely different path. A friend of hers who was a fan of the reality cable show *Trading Spaces*—based on the British show *Changing Rooms*—learned that the show's host had quit after one season, and urged Davis to audition for the position. In spite of the fact that the bulk of her experience was in theater and not television, the producers of *Trading Spaces* were impressed by Davis's enthusiasm and sparkling personality, and they hired her on as host beginning with the 2001 season.

In each episode of *Trading Spaces,* neighbors swap house keys for two days to redesign one room in each others' homes. The show provides a budget of $1,000 for each family as well as assistance from professional designers and carpenters. The homeowners do much of the physical work themselves, painting walls, wallpapering, and staining woodwork. As the show's host, Davis introduces the participants to viewers at the beginning of each episode, explaining their relationship to each other and pointing out the design challenges for the rooms that will undergo transformation. She then takes viewers through the highlights of the renovation, focusing not only on the physical changes to the room but also on the emotional discomfort the participants feel as they wonder how their neighbors will react to their work and what the redesigned room in their own house will look like. When needed, Davis even pitches in with the manual labor. She told Huisking, "I'm 100 percent invested in what the designers want and what the homeowners are feeling. When I'm not on camera, I'm having lunch with the homeowners, hearing about their children, helping them paint, trying to make them as relaxed as possible."

The high point of each episode is what's known as the "reveal," when the homeowners are guided, eyes shut, to the newly redesigned room in their home to see what their neighbors have done. Reactions range from joy to puzzlement to downright horror, with some homeowners breaking down in tears when they see the changes made to their room. While she knows some television viewers especially enjoy the homeowners' negative reactions, Davis is too personally involved in each renovation experience to derive pleasure from these occasions. "It does make good television," she acknowledged to Thomas Nord of the Louisville, Kentucky, *Courier-Journal.* "I have friends who tell me they love it when that happens. I hate it. It's terribly awkward and sad."

In her spare time

In 2003 Davis published *Paige by Paige: A Year of Trading Spaces,* a behind-the-scenes account of one season of the show. In the book Davis describes the mishaps and blunders that sometimes occur off-camera. She recounts the adventures she has had with the cast and crew during their travels, and inserts tidbits about the personalities of the designers and others who work on the show. Her recollections include some of the more memorable homeowner reactions of the season, including the Las Vegas resident who refused to speak to her neighbors after seeing the color they had chosen to paint her room. After participating in the redesign of more than two hundred rooms, Davis told Stephanie Schorow of the *Boston Herald* that she wanted to renovate her own apartment in Manhattan. "It's very predictable," she said of her current design scheme. "I want to be more brave."

Paige Davis poses outside the Ambassador Theatre in New York City, where she appeared in the musical **Chicago.** AP/Wide World Photos. Reproduced by permission.

Davis has alternated her *Trading Spaces* duties with occasional returns to her first love: the theater. She spent a week in May of 2003 performing in the traveling production of Eve Ensler's provocative work *The Vagina Monologues,* and during the summer of 2004 she headlined the Broadway production of *Chicago,* starring in the role she had previously understudied: that of Roxie Hart. While she may never have envisioned herself as host of a reality home improvement program, Davis has expressed unflagging enthusiasm for her work. She told Sandra Kallio of the *Wisconsin State Journal,* "It's remarkable what happens every single time. It blows my mind."

For More Information

Periodicals

Huisking, Charlie. "Paige Davis Finds Space for Theater." *Sarasota (FL) Herald Tribune* (May 13, 2003): p. E1.

Kallio, Sandra. "She Wouldn't Trade Places." *Wisconsin State Journal* (August 20, 2003): p. D1.

Nord, Thomas. *Louisville (KY) Courier-Journal* (August 6, 2002): p. 1C.

Schorow, Stephanie. "Diary Opens Window into World of Home Makeover Host." *Boston Herald* (August 17, 2003): p. 49.

Web sites

"Trading Spaces." *TLC.com.* http://tlc.discovery.com/fansites/trading-spaces/tradingspaces.html (accessed May 12, 2004).

Paige Davis Official Web site. http://www.paigedavis.com (accessed May 12, 2004).

Ellen DeGeneres

January 26, 1958 • *Metairie, Louisiana*

Comedian, actress, author

Ellen DeGeneres is one of the most popular contemporary comedians and the host of a successful daytime talk show. She is perhaps best known to young audiences as the voice of the endearing but absent-minded fish Dory in the blockbuster animated hit *Finding Nemo* (2003), a role that perfectly captured her rambling, seemingly unrehearsed comic style. After rising through the ranks of stand-up comedy during the 1980s and early 1990s, DeGeneres became a successful television star with her show *Ellen* in the mid-1990s. Her career became temporarily derailed in the late 1990s, but she got back on track a few years later, surpassing her earlier successes by a long shot. During 2003 DeGeneres published a best-selling book of short stories and essays, toured across the United States with a new stand-up routine, voiced the part of Dory in *Finding Nemo,* and launched her syndicated talk show. Displaying the self-assurance that comes from a string of successful career moves, DeGeneres explained to Nicholas Fonseca of *Entertainment Weekly* how she feels about her latest venture: "I've never been so passionate about something. I will probably do this for the rest of my career."

A late-blooming comedian

DeGeneres was born outside New Orleans and spent most of her childhood there, living with her parents and her older brother, Vance. As a child, DeGeneres spent much of her free time exploring the city. She recalled to Liz Scott of *New Orleans Magazine,* "I rode my bike everywhere. All over the campus [of Newcomb College]. All over uptown. You know, people can grow up in New Orleans without realizing how unique a city it is. I remember thinking that it was a really neat place."

> "I'm doing a talk show. It's not my job to get into an argument with somebody about religion or politics or sexuality or anything. It is my job to make people laugh."

When DeGeneres was thirteen years old, her parents divorced, and she moved with her mother to Atlanta, Texas. As quoted in the *St. James Encyclopedia of Popular Culture,* she recalled using comedy to help her mother through the painful period after the divorce: "My mother was going through some really hard times and I could see when she was really getting down, and I would start to make fun of her dancing," DeGeneres remembered. "Then she'd start to laugh and I'd make fun of her laughing. And she'd laugh so hard she'd start to cry, and then I'd make fun of that. So I would totally bring her from where I'd seen her start going into depression to all the way out of it."

After DeGeneres graduated from high school in 1976, she moved back to New Orleans, holding down a series of jobs, none of which suited her personality. She worked for a time in a law firm but felt stifled by the dress code. She held a number of restaurant jobs, from hostess to bartender to oyster shucker. She also worked at a retail clothing store and as a house painter. Ultimately she realized that she did not like following other people's rules, and she would have to make a career for herself that allowed for independence. At the age of twenty-three, she started to flesh out a comedy routine, first performing just for friends and then at local coffeehouses and comedy clubs. Soon she became the master of ceremonies, or emcee, at a New Orleans comedy club. In 1982 she entered a national talent contest held by the cable network Showtime, sending in a videotape of her stand-up act. When DeGeneres won the contest, earning the title of "Funniest Person in America," she went immediately from local New Orleans comic to nationally recognized up-and-coming comedian. Over the next several years, she traveled around the country performing stand-up comedy, and she appeared on several HBO specials.

In 1986 DeGeneres made history in her first-ever appearance on the *Tonight Show Starring Johnny Carson.* Most comedians who appeared on the *Tonight Show* performed their stand-up routine and then returned backstage, never being invited to sit on the couch and have an on-camera chat with Carson. The invitation to sit down with Carson paid tribute to a comedian's talent and stature. A female comedian had never been asked to sit on the couch after a first-time performance on the show. The night DeGeneres debuted on the *Tonight Show* in 1986, Carson brought her over to the couch. She had arrived.

Breaking ground

In 1991 DeGeneres was honored as best female stand-up comic at the 1991 American Comedy Awards. About the same time, she branched out to begin acting in television series. She appeared in a couple of short-lived sitcoms, *Open House* and *Laurie Hill,* before earning her own show. *These Friends of Mine* premiered on ABC in March of 1994, receiving mixed reviews and decent ratings. The show starred DeGeneres as Ellen Morgan, an employee (and later owner) of a bookstore called Buy the Book. It focused on the lives of Ellen and her friends, finding humor in the mundane, everyday events of the characters' lives. By the beginning of the second season, the show had undergone major changes, including its title, which became *Ellen.* The reviews and the ratings steadily improved, as more and more viewers connected with DeGeneres's oddball humor and appealing, average-gal persona. DeGeneres earned numerous nominations for Emmy Awards, and in 1997 she won the prestigious Peabody Award for her work on the show.

In the spring of 1997, DeGeneres made pop-culture history by having her character come out as a lesbian, becoming the first gay lead character on a network television sitcom. That show, called "The Puppy Episode," garnered forty-six million viewers and brought DeGeneres an Emmy Award for best comedy writing. At the same time, DeGeneres herself came out to millions with a cover story in *Time* magazine announcing that she is gay. The announcement came as no surprise—fans and journalists had speculated that it was coming—but it still generated a media storm. Many fans wrote supportive letters, while others were scandalized by the news. During the 1997–98 season, *Ellen* began losing viewers. Many observers suggested that the show had fundamentally changed when the main character's sexual orientation became the focus of numerous episodes. Some believed that the network simply did not want the controversy generated by the announcement about Ellen's sexuality. Some major advertisers had pulled out, and the network, fearful of offending viewers, began attaching warning labels to episodes that showed Ellen kissing another woman or discussing her sexual orientation. The show was cancelled after the 1997–98 season.

After her show's cancellation, DeGeneres went through a difficult period, both professionally and personally. Her highly publicized relationship and August of 2000 breakup with actress Anne Heche (1969–) eroded much of the goodwill fans felt toward her—or at least that is what DeGeneres believed, as she explained in an article in *People* magazine: "I went through a phase, whether it was true or not, where my perception was, 'Everyone hates me now,' and it felt horrible." She appeared in a number of films during this period, including *EDtv* and *The Love Letter,* but none of these established her as a successful film actress. In 2001 DeGeneres starred in a short-lived sitcom called *The Ellen Show,* which was praised by reviewers but never attracted a large audience.

Amid these disappointments, DeGeneres's professional life hit one distinctly positive note, setting the stage for what some have described as her career's second act. Soon after the terrorist attacks of September 11, 2001, DeGeneres was asked to host the prime-time Emmy Awards, a program that had been delayed twice due to the

tragedy. As many in the entertainment industry struggled over how to amuse audiences—or whether they should even try—in the somber aftermath of 9/11, DeGeneres impressed her fellow actors and millions of viewers with what Fonseca described in *Entertainment Weekly* as a "witty, respectful, and wise" performance.

From left, Christiana Aquilera, Molly Shannon, and Ellen Degeneres, during a taping of **The Ellen Degeneres Show.** AP/Wide World Photos. Reproduced by permission.

Finding her audience—again

Over the next year or so, DeGeneres began showing up on television more and more often. She hosted *Saturday Night Live,* appeared on an episode of *Will and Grace,* and occupied the center square on the primetime game show *Hollywood Squares.* Suddenly, in 2003, DeGeneres was everywhere. She returned to stand-up with a hugely successful thirty-five-city tour, culminating with an HBO comedy special called *Ellen DeGeneres: Here and Now.* She published a best-selling book of comic essays called *The Funny Thing Is...,* and she lent her voice to what became the highest-grossing animated movie of all time: Disney/Pixar's *Finding Nemo.* The character of the blue tang fish Dory seemed tailor-made for DeGeneres's wide-eyed, naive, and intensely likable persona, and in fact the role was written expressly for her. In a September of 2003 article in *Entertainment Weekly,* Andrew Stanton, the film's director and cowriter, explained why DeGeneres was his only choice for that character: "Everybody has that friend who's funny merely for existing. That's Ellen. You're not waiting for a punchline with her. You're just waiting for her to speak so you can start laughing."

In the fall of 2003, DeGeneres found herself once again at the center of a self-titled television program; this time she was not the star of a sitcom but the host of a syndicated daytime talk show. In its first season, *The Ellen DeGeneres Show* earned positive reviews and solid ratings across the nation. The successful year was topped off with a record twelve Emmy Award nominations in 2004, the most ever received by a talk show in its debut season. According to an article in the *Washington Post,* when she heard the news about the Emmy nominations, DeGeneres responded with a comment typical of her self-criticizing, slightly insecure comedic style: "They told me, you got nominations for every single category except the song, and I instantly said, 'What's wrong with our song?'" In addition to three technical awards, DeGeneres's program won the 2004 Emmy for outstanding talk show. Basking in a post-Emmy glow, DeGeneres commented in an article at *CNN.com:* "I have fun every day. It's the best job I ever had."

The joys of DeGeneres's professional successes are underscored by her stable and happy personal life. She has spent several years in a relationship with photographer and actress Alexandra Hedison. The two share a home on a three-acre spread in the Hollywood Hills. In a late 2003 article in *People,* DeGeneres reflected on her career, concluding that both the highs and the lows have been valuable to her: "Right now I'm in such a good place, and I'm so grateful for every step of the way, because it makes me appreciate this time even more."

For More Information

Books

St. James Encyclopedia of Popular Culture. 5 vols. Detroit: St. James Press, 2000.

Periodicals

Blumenstock, Kathy. "DeGeneres Attempts to Give Her Viewers a 'Sense of Fun.'" *Washington Post* (May 16, 2004).

Fonseca, Nicholas. "The New Queen of Nice." *Entertainment Weekly* (September 12, 2003): p. 112.

Scott, Liz. "Ellen DeGeneres." *New Orleans Magazine* (July 1994): p. 68.

Tauber, Michelle, and Julie Jordan. "Look Who's Talking." *People* (November 10, 2003): p. 93.

Web Sites

"DeGeneres, Brady among Daytime Emmy Winners." *CNN.com.* http://www.cnn.com/2004/SHOWBIZ/TV/05/22/daytime.emmys.ap/ (accessed on June 26, 2004).

The Ellen DeGeneres Show. http://ellen.warnerbros.com/ (accessed on June 26, 2004).

Michael Dell

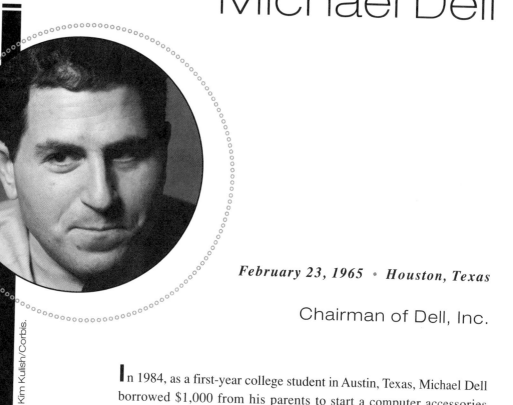

February 23, 1965 • Houston, Texas

Chairman of Dell, Inc.

In 1984, as a first-year college student in Austin, Texas, Michael Dell borrowed $1,000 from his parents to start a computer accessories business. He began by selling kits to help customers upgrade their personal computers, establishing a business model his company, Dell, Inc., still follows today: sell directly to consumers, eliminating the middle step of a retail store or a distributor, and hold on to far more of the profits. In just two decades, Dell's company grew to massive proportions, with more than 47,000 employees and annual revenues of more than $40 billion. Dell himself was squarely at the top of *Forbes* magazine's list of the ten wealthiest Americans under the age of forty. He has been praised as a visionary and an innovator, but he has also earned admiration for being a stable, consistent leader. In an industry that changes rapidly, in terms of both technology and personnel, Dell has stood out from his peers by remaining at the helm of his company from its struggling early days to its current status as a major player in the global field of information technology (IT).

A businessman from the beginning

Michael Saul Dell was born in 1965 in Houston, Texas. While he displayed intelligence and ingenuity from an early age, he had little interest in school. At the age of eight, he sent away for information on taking a high school equivalency exam, which, if he passed, would make him a high school graduate without having to endure the remaining years of school. His parents insisted he stay in the classroom, and Dell invested his considerable creative energy in afterschool ventures. When he was twelve years old, he operated a mail-order trading business for stamps and baseball cards, earning $2,000. At the age of fourteen, Dell got his first computer, an Apple II and

> **"What people have never understood is that we're not like other companies."**

soon realized that he had a knack for taking computers apart and putting them back together. While in high school, Dell took a job delivering newspapers for the *Houston Post*. His aggressive selling strategies—which included obtaining mailing lists of newly married people, offering them free trial subscriptions, and then following up with phone calls—resulted in earnings of $18,000. Not one to hold on to his spoils, Dell spent the money on a new BMW.

In 1983, when Dell entered his freshman year at the University of Texas at Austin, his parents hoped he would become a doctor, but Dell's skills lay elsewhere. In examining the personal computer, or PC, industry, he noticed an opportunity to sell PCs for less, as he explained to Richard Murphy of *Success* magazine: "I saw that you'd buy a PC for about $3,000, and inside that PC was about $600 worth of parts. IBM would buy most of these parts from other companies, assemble them, and sell the computer to a dealer for $2,000. Then the dealer, who knew very little about selling or supporting computers, would sell it for $3,000, which was even more outrageous." Dell realized that he could assemble computer parts, skip the step of selling to a dealer, and go directly to the consumer. That way the consumer could buy the product for less, and Dell held on to every penny of the profits. Dell thus combined his knowledge of computers with his well-developed business sense and began his own business, assembling upgrade kits for personal computers.

In a 1999 article in *Fortune,* Dell recalled operating his new business out of his University of Texas dorm room on the twenty-seventh floor: "People would ride up to the 27th floor with their computers. I'd put in some memory or a disk drive, they'd pay me, and I'd send them on their way." His earnings soon reached about $25,000 a month. By the summer of 1984, after one year at the university, Dell had decided that he needed to focus all of his time on his business, and he dropped out of college. His company, then called PCs Unlimited, began building PCs, starting with parts from such established computer companies as IBM and Compaq and adding elements to make the products unique. Dell continued to sell directly to consumers, a strategy that paid off in vast sums: by the end of 1984, his company had earned $6 million. Dell was off and running, leading his company to enormous growth year after year.

Michael Dell answers a call from a customer. AP/Wide World Photo. Reproduced by permission.

The envy of CEOs everywhere

By early 1985, at the age of twenty, Dell had thirty employees working for him. During the summer of that year, the company began producing the Turbo PC, its first computer made entirely from scratch, rather than a customized version of another company's machine. In 1987 Dell changed the name of the company from PCs Unlimited to Dell Computer Corporation. At that time he began a program offered by no one else in the industry: rather than having customers bring broken-down computers to a store for repair, Dell Computer would pay house calls to service its customers' PCs. In *Success* magazine, Dell pointed out that this offer came out of necessity rather than an ingenious plan to outperform competitors: "That was a pretty important plus because we didn't have any stores," he recalled. During 1988 Dell began offering the public the opportunity to buy stock in his company. Just four years after the company had begun, sales reached

A Brief History of Personal Computers

For many people, it is nearly impossible to imagine life without computers, yet it was not long ago that computers were a rare item, seen perhaps by the average citizen only on television. Mainframe computers of the 1950s took up entire rooms; minicomputers were the size of refrigerators; and microcomputers, which eventually became known as personal computers (PCs), could fit on a desktop. Today, many varieties of wireless computers can be held in the palm of a hand.

In the early 1970s, consumer demand for home and business computers began to develop. About that time, Ed Roberts, owner Micro Instrumentation Telemetry Systems (MITS), worked with engineers to develop the MITS Altair 8800. This computer was sold as a kit for $400; it had to be assembled by the consumer, who also had to write the software. In spite of these hurdles, MITS was flooded with orders for the Altair in 1975. Soon after the Altair hit the market, two young programmers approached Roberts to inform him of an existing software program that could be adapted to work on the Altair. These programmers, Paul Allen and Bill Gates, then a first-year student at Harvard University, created a version of the program, called BASIC, for the Altair. Later, MITS went out of business, and Gates and Allen founded Microsoft, the global software giant.

In about 1973 Xerox developed the Alto, a computer featuring a mouse and a point-and-click graphical user interface (GUI). The company never marketed this computer to the public, however, as Xerox management could not envision how consumers would use it. Computers that featured a GUI, including Apple's Lisa and Macintosh models, did not become widespread for another ten years. In 1975 Steve Wozniak and Steve Jobs, two computer hobbyists, began working together to build their own PC using inexpensive parts. The following year they founded Apple Computers and released the Apple I. In 1977 Apple Computers released the Apple II, considered by many to be the first true personal computer. This PC, which

$159 million. Dell found success in his personal life at that time, too; he married Susan Lieberman in October of 1989. Residing in Austin's hill country, the couple has four children.

Dell Computer grew at an astronomical rate, and with that growth came problems. During 1993 the industry as a whole was suffering a slowdown, with consumers buying fewer PCs. Dell Computer was suffering from numerous management problems. The company scrapped plans for a new laptop computer when it realized the product was outmatched by its competitors. An attempt to sell Dell computers through retail outlets like Best Buy and Wal-Mart had failed. Recognizing that his company needed to be overhauled, Dell brought in several new high-level managers with years of experience in high-tech industries. Many of the day-to-day responsibilities were delegated to these trusted executives, leaving Dell to concentrate on the company's

sold for just under $1,300, featured color graphics and a disk drive. Apple's primary competitor was Commodore, which released the Commodore PET in early 1977. The PET had features similar to Apple II but was sold for half the price. Commodore also created the Commodore 64, which featured a good deal of memory and color graphics and used inexpensive floppy disks for storing files. The Commodore 64 became the best-selling PC of all time.

Computers were catching on with a small segment of the population, but it was not until the invention of spreadsheet software in 1979 that many businesses saw the benefits of using PCs. With the development of VisiCalc, a program invented by Dan Bricklin and Bob Frankston, businesses calculating their finances could use computer software to perform in a few minutes tasks that had previously taken hours. When a user changed one number in a column, the software automatically calculated the change to every other number on the sheet, changes that otherwise had to be done by hand. During that same year, Wordstar, a groundbreaking word-processing software, was released and became immedi-ately successful. With Wordstar and similar software, users could create, edit, save, and print documents using their computers.

With the release of the IBM PC—the computer credited with popularizing the phrase "personal computer"—in August of 1981, the PC came to be seen as a vital business tool and a machine that could be useful to general consumers as well. The IBM PC was designed with an open architecture, meaning that similar computers built by other companies could use IBM software. Microsoft, first with the development of MS-DOS and later with Windows, became the primary developer of operating systems—the programs that run every other program on a computer—for IBM-type PCs. While Apple had popularized computers with graphical user interfaces, Microsoft became a major GUI player with the release of its first Windows operating system in 1985. Developments in the personal computer since that time have been less dramatic than in the early years, focusing primarily on increasing memory, speed, and portability, decreasing the machine's size, and improving the quality of the GUI.

overall vision and strategy. The reorganization helped the company regain its footing, a triumph marked by the hugely successful release of a new laptop computer, the Latitude XP.

Many business analysts have suggested that one of Dell's secrets to success has been his ability to remain focused on his winning business model: sell directly to consumers, keep prices low and quality high, and offer solid technological support to customers. Within thirty-six hours of a customer ordering a PC by phone or through the company's Web site, a custom-built Dell computer is shipped. To keep its costs down, the company maintains an extremely low inventory of computer parts, at any given time housing only enough components to fulfill a few days' worth of orders. This strategy not only reduces the need for warehouse space but also ensures that, in the rapidly changing computer industry, Dell always has in stock the newest parts its suppliers offer. Michael Dell has been able to maintain his company's steady growth rate by selling not just to individual consumers but also to large corporations, educational institutions, and government agencies. The company has expanded its line of products in recent years to include network servers (powerful machines that run computer networks), storage systems, handheld computers, and printers—an expansion signified by its 2003 name change from Dell Computer to Dell, Inc. Dell has extended its customer base throughout the world, most notably into Asia, capturing 7 percent of the PC market in China by 2004.

During the summer of 2004, Dell, who had been chairman and chief executive officer, or CEO, of his company, relinquished the CEO position, passing that title on to Kevin Rollins, his former president and chief operating officer. In a 2004 interview with *Fortune* magazine, Dell and Rollins stated that the change in their job titles did not signal any major shift in the way the company would be run. Dell declared: "We run the business together, and we're going to continue." Since its beginnings in 1984, the company has set a rapid pace for growth; it took Dell just twenty years to surpass industry leader Hewlett-Packard to hold the largest share of the computer-making market. A 2001 article in *The Economist* summed up Dell's accomplishment, stating, "There is hardly a more admired boss than Mr. Dell, the man who turned the commodity business of PC making into a goldmine by doing things differently."

For More Information

Periodicals

Calonius, Erik. "Their Wildest Dreams." *Fortune* (August 16, 1999): p. 142.

Kirkpatrick, David. "Dell and Robbins: The $41 Billion Buddy Act." *Fortune* (April 19, 2004): p. 84.

Murphy, Richard. "Michael Dell." *Success* (January 1999): p. 50.

"A Revolution of One." *The Economist* (April 14, 2001): p. 10.

Web Sites

"Dell Inc." *Hoover's Online.* http://www.hoovers.com/dell/—ID__13193—/free-co-factsheet.xhtml (accessed on June 26, 2004).

"Executive Biographies: Michael S. Dell." *Dell.* http://www1.us.dell.com/content/topics/global.aspx/corp/biographies/en/michael_dell?c=us&l=;en&s=corp (accessed on June 26, 2004).

Hilary Duff

September 28, 1987 • Houston, Texas

Actress, singer

Young teens everywhere first came to know Hilary Duff as Lizzie McGuire, the title character of the Disney Channel show that aired from 2001 until 2003. As Lizzie, Duff played an awkward, slightly clumsy junior high schooler—a bit of a stretch for the confident, multitalented actress. Since establishing a successful television career with *Lizzie McGuire,* Duff has branched out to conquer multiple fronts: she has acted in a number of feature films, including starring roles in *The Lizzie McGuire Movie* and *A Cinderella Story;* she has released her own album, *Metamorphosis*; and she presides over a line of clothing, makeup, and accessories, called Stuff by Hilary Duff. Duff accomplished all of this before her seventeenth birthday, but in spite of her rapid ascent to fame, she works hard to remain grounded, helped along by close relationships with her family and friends.

Texas girl heads to Hollywood

Duff was born in Houston, Texas, far from the glitter and glamour of Los Angeles. She knew from a young age, however, that she enjoyed performing. She studied gymnastics and ballet, and when her older sister, Haylie, began taking acting lessons, Hilary joined her. At age six Duff joined a touring production of *The Nutcracker* ballet, and she also acted in local commercials as a youngster. She earned her first television role in 1996, in the miniseries *True Women,* which aired the following year.

Once Haylie and Hilary began getting acting jobs, they persuaded their parents that they had to live in Los Angeles if they were to

> **"I get zits and bad hair just like everyone else. But I think you have to work through it. I'm very into embracing your flaws and knowing that you're beautiful for a lot of different reasons besides just what you look like on the outside."**

have any chance at a career in the entertainment industry. During the late 1990s, despite her declaration in *Newsweek* that she "never wanted to be a stage mom," Susan Duff drove her daughters, their possessions, and their pets from Texas to Los Angeles. The girls' father, Bob, stayed in Texas—he is a partner in a convenience-store chain—but he flies to California every few weeks to spend time with his family. Soon after the move, Duff hit the audition circuit, trying out for every part she could find. She was cast as Wendy in the direct-to-video film *Casper Meets Wendy* in 1998. She earned a role in the television movie *The Soul Collector* and a guest appearance on *Chicago Hope.* Then, in 2000, Duff auditioned for the Disney Channel's upcoming new show, *Lizzie McGuire.* After appearing before the show's producers four times, Duff was hired. Rich Ross, president of the Disney channel's entertainment division, commented in *Newsweek* on the number of try-

Amanda Bynes Makes the Transition

Amanda Bynes (1986–), a standout among the crop of young stars getting their start on television shows aimed at the tween audience, spent several years sharpening her comedic skills on the Nickelodeon network before successfully heading to the big screen. Born in 1986 and raised in the Los Angeles area, Bynes entered show business at a young age. She was discovered while participating in a children's comedy workshop at the age of seven, and by her tenth birthday she had been hired as part of the cast of Nickelodeon's *All That.* During her four years on that sketch comedy show, Bynes displayed her sharp comic timing and physical comedy chops. The network felt her potential was so great that she earned her own show in 1999, *The Amanda Show.* Both shows highlighted Bynes's facility for goofy humor; *Time*'s Richard Corliss wrote of comparisons made between Bynes and two highly respected queens of comedy: "She has been called the new Lucille Ball and the next Gilda Radner, thanks to her deft, daft turns on [Nickelodeon]." Bynes attracted a large following, particularly among preteen viewers. She was voted favorite television actress three years in a row on Nickelodeon's Kids' Choice awards.

While Bynes enjoyed the years of silly wigs and outrageous pratfalls, she longed for the opportunity to be viewed as a legitimate actress. Knowing she eventually wanted to make the transition to more challenging roles, preferably on the big screen, Bynes waited until she was well into her teen years before pursuing that goal. She appeared opposite Frankie Muniz in the 2002 film *Big Fat Liar,* and later that year she earned a starring role in a new sitcom on the WB, *What I Like about You.* Costarring Jennie Garth, formerly of *Beverly Hills 90210,* the series features Bynes as a suburban teen who moves in with her city-dwelling older sister. In 2003 she scored a headlining role in *What a Girl Wants,* a modern-day retelling of the 1958 hit *The Reluctant Debutante.* Bynes plays a free-spirited American girl who jets off to London to find her father, an aristocratic Englishman who does not even know she exists. While the film received mixed reviews, many critics were struck by Bynes's fresh-faced appeal and easy on-camera confidence. *What a Girl Wants* served as an effective launching pad for Bynes, who began entertaining numerous other film offers soon after its release.

Like her fellow teen queen Hilary Duff, Bynes has retained a down-to-earth outlook amidst her international stardom. She has expressed a desire to have a long-term acting career, but she has little interest in the glitzy entertainment-industry scene. Bynes told Corliss: "I pride myself on not being Hollywood. I could go to the parties and stuff, but for me it's so fake."

outs: "She wasn't doing anything wrong. She just wore such great outfits, and we wanted to see what she'd come in with next."

Life as Lizzie

Lizzie McGuire began airing in 2001, when both Duff and the character she played were thirteen years old. On the show, Lizzie—sweet, smart, but not terribly smooth—encounters problems typical for a girl navigating the treacherous waters of adolescence: crushes on boys, arguments with friends, and difficulties with parents. While Lizzie sometimes fumbles her way through crisis situations, the cartoon version of Lizzie, who appears periodically to comment on the circumstances, always knows just what to say and do. The show quickly became a huge success, earning a massive following among tween girls—that is, girls between the ages of about eight and fourteen—and even among older teens and people in their twenties. Parents approved of the show for its positive outlook, and kids loved *Lizzie* because it portrayed the problems of a normal, average girl. The show's executive producer, Stan Rogow, told *Entertainment Weekly*'s Tim Carvell that Lizzie was characterized "by what she wasn't: She wasn't the cheerleader, she wasn't the diva, she wasn't the jock, she just was Lizzie."

Watching "just Lizzie" week after week was more than enough for viewers, who adored the character as well as the actress who played her. Duff became a celebrity almost overnight; she could hardly go anywhere without encountering young fans who wanted her autograph or a photo. Famous for playing a typical teen, Duff suddenly had a life that was far from typical. Rather than go to school, she worked with an on-set tutor several hours a day. In addition to filming episodes of *Lizzie McGuire,* Duff also branched out to film roles, playing young Lila Jute in *Human Nature* in 2001 and the title role in the 2002 television movie *Cadet Kelly.* At this time she also began expanding her career to include singing, recording "I Can't Wait," the opening track for the *Lizzie McGuire* show. She contributed a track to the CD *Disneymania,* and she (along with several featured guests) released a Christmas album in 2002, *Santa Claus Lane.*

Triple threat

Two thousand three was a banner year for Duff, when she made the transition from Disney-bred tween sensation to bona fide star of television, films, and pop music. *Lizzie McGuire* continued as the Disney Channel's number-one series, spawning the equally successful *Lizzie McGuire Movie,* which features Lizzie heading to Rome for a summertime class trip. While there, she meets a handsome Italian singer named Paolo and is persuaded to assume the identity of pop star Isabella, Paolo's partner, who happens to be a dead ringer for young

Lizzie. In addition to starring in the film, Duff recorded several songs for the hit soundtrack. Also during 2003, Duff had a starring role opposite fellow television actor Frankie Muniz (1985–) in the movie *Agent Cody Banks,* in which she plays Natalie, Cody Banks's love interest. The year was capped off with a role as one of the twelve children in *Cheaper by the Dozen,* starring Steve Martin (1945–).

Duff's whirlwind success encountered an obstacle when she and Disney parted ways during the negotiations for a sequel to *The Lizzie McGuire Movie.* The television series was in its final season, with Disney limiting it to sixty-five episodes, and when the two parties were unable to reach a deal for a second movie, Duff faced a Lizzie-less future.

Although *Lizzie* fans were heartbroken, the effect on Duff's career proved minimal. She continued to score film roles, starring in both *A Cinderella Story* and *Raise Your Voice* in 2004. She also made a successful transition from actress to pop singer, releasing her first full-length solo album, *Metamorphosis,* in August of 2003. By October of that year, the album had gone platinum, meaning one million copies had sold. Three months later, that number had nearly tripled. The executives at her label, Buena Vista (which is owned by Disney), made it a priority to market Duff's music not just to her preteen *Lizzie* fans but also to an older audience. The songs were crafted by a team of veteran pop songwriters and producers; however, two tracks were written by a relative newcomer: Duff's big sister, Haylie.

Hillary Duff performs at the Universal Amphitheatre in 2004. © Lucia DeMasi/Corbis.

Crucial to the acceptance of Duff as more than just a tween queen was her presence on MTV, as noted by Craig Rosen in *Billboard*: "The Disney Channel show *Lizzie McGuire* may have launched Duff's career, but MTV has been influential in helping her make the transformation from TV personality to pop star." The video for the album's hit single "So Yesterday" reached number two on *Total Request Live (TRL),* MTV's must-see all-request show. The video of another single, "Why Not," also appeared regularly on *TRL.* Another important partner helping Duff find musical success was America Online, or AOL, which offered its Internet subscribers exclu-

sive and abundant access to Duff videos, concerts, photos, and more. *Metamorphosis* found success in more conventional channels as well: "So Yesterday," for example, made a huge splash on Top 40 radio and reached number one on *Billboard*'s Hot 100 chart.

Marketing and merchandise

In November of 2003 Duff expanded her territory even farther, releasing a DVD called *All Access Pass*. Her first music DVD, *All Access Pass* includes videos for the singles "So Yesterday," "I Can't Wait," and "Why Not." It also features footage of live performances as well as behind-the-scenes glimpses of Duff and her creative team hard at work. The fall of 2003 also saw the release of three Hilary Duff fashion dolls, each of which represents a facet of Duff's career: rock star, movie star, and TV star. The following spring, Duff premiered her own line of clothing, shoes, cosmetics, and accessories; Stuff by Hilary Duff is sold at Target in the United States and by other retailers elsewhere, including Zellers in Canada and Kmart in Australia.

Going well beyond a simple acting and singing career, Duff presides over a multimedia empire. In spite of having grown up in front of a camera, Duff has managed, according to family and friends, to remain a sincere, down-to-earth person. In *Entertainment Weekly, Lizzie McGuire* executive producer Rogow gave much of the credit to Duff's parents, acknowledging the dangers of allowing a child into show business: "It takes an extraordinary effort, I think, to avoid [the pitfalls]. It's a full-time thing … and somehow, the Duffs have been able to do it." In an attempt to use her fame to change the world, Duff is active in Kids with a Cause, a nonprofit organization that helps combat poverty, illness, and neglect among young people. An animal lover, she is also involved with a wild horse sanctuary called Return to Freedom. Duff has expressed a true appreciation for what she has achieved, showing no signs of taking her success for granted. In a 2004 interview with *CosmoGirl!* magazine, she looked back on her pre-*Lizzie* days and gave credit to the whole Duff clan: "I've worked really hard—and it hasn't been just me. It's been a team effort with my entire family, including my sister, Haylie. Over the last five years, I auditioned and auditioned and kept trying and trying, and now we're seeing the reward for all the work we did."

For More Information

Periodicals

Berger, Lori. "Hilary Duff." *CosmoGirl!* (March 2004): p. 126.

Carvell, Tim. "The Girl in the Bubble." *Entertainment Weekly* (May 9, 2003): p. 34.

Corliss, Richard. "The Fresh-Face Factory." *Time* (April 14, 2003): p. 76.

Rosen, Craig. "Hilary Duff: A Performer's Metamorphosis." *Billboard* (January 31, 2004): p. 10.

Stroup, Kate. "Girl Power." *Newsweek* (March 17, 2003): p. 56.

Web Sites

Hilary Duff. http://www.hilaryduff.com/html_2003/main_site/frameset.htm (accessed on June 26, 2004).

Hilary Duff: Metamorphosis. http://buenavistarecords.go.com/hilaryduff/ (accessed on June 26, 2004).

Dale Earnhardt Jr.

October 10, 1974 • *Kannapolis, North Carolina*

Race-car driver

Dale Earnhardt Jr. possesses one of the most familiar names—and faces—in the world of stock-car racing, but he has yet to become a top-ranked champion driver for the National Association for Stock Car Auto Racing, better known as NASCAR. Much of his fame stems from his family name: he is the son of the late Dale Earnhardt, one of NASCAR's most beloved stars. Since his father's death from a crash during the 2001 Daytona 500, the younger Earnhardt has had to make his own way: as a driver, as a grieving son, and as a celebrity. He has won several major races in NASCAR's premier racing series, the Nextel Cup (formerly known as the Winston Cup), including the Daytona 500 in February of 2004. Earnhardt is one of NASCAR's most popular drivers. He has a devoted following among race fans, many of whom started out as fans of his father. However, Earnhardt has, in his own right, captured the hearts of millions with his racing talent as well as his easygoing, regular-guy personality.

A racing dynasty

Earnhardt was born into a racing family. His father, Dale Sr., known as the Intimidator, was a seven-time Winston Cup champion and winner of seventy-six races in a career that spanned more than twenty years. Dale Sr. went into racing to follow in his own father's footsteps; Ralph Earnhardt was the 1956 champion of the NASCAR National Sportsman division, now known as the Busch series. "I wanted to race—that's all I ever wanted to do," Dale Sr. proclaimed in a profile of the Earnhardts at *NASCAR.com*. Dale Jr. clearly inherited his father's passion as well as the racing mentality and incorporated it into his own life. At *NASCAR.com* Dale Sr. recalled taking his son go-

> **"There's nothing better and nothing I'd rather do than be going around the track in a race car. That's something I've fallen in love with and don't want to give up for a long time."**

karting when the boy was about ten years old. At one point as he raced around the track, Dale Jr.'s wheel was clipped, the go-kart spun out of control, and the boy went flying. His concerned father raced across the track, but the boy jumped up and immediately asked about his go-kart. Dale Sr. recalled, "The only thing he was concerned about was 'Where's my go-kart?' That was a pretty awesome sight, I'll tell you."

The lure of racing was so powerful in the Earnhardt family that Dale Jr., his sister, Kelley, and his half-brother, Kerry, all entered the sport. Kelley Earnhardt told Lee Spencer of the *Sporting News* that when they were growing up together she would not have guessed that her brother, Dale Jr., would become a racer: "He spent a lot of time playing with Matchbox cars, but he was not aggressive … and didn't take risks." At first Earnhardt joined another branch of the family business, going to work at his father's Chevrolet dealership. However, by his late teens he had begun racing. Earnhardt and his brother Kerry pooled their resources to buy a 1978 Monte Carlo, which they rebuilt and raced in the Street Stock division. After two seasons, Earnhardt moved up to the Late Model division, in which he raced for three seasons. In 113 races in that division between 1994 and 1996, he won only three times, but he astounded onlookers by finishing in the top ten ninety times. His relationship to his legendary father earned him no special treatment during the early years; the teenager used his own money and was expected to secure his own corporate sponsors, companies that help finance a racer in exchange for the display of their logo on the car or on the driver's uniform. Just as his father had done, Dale Earnhardt Jr. had to work his way up.

By 1997 Earnhardt had done just that, moving up to NASCAR's more prestigious Busch series. At that point, everything changed. "I was having fun driving late-model cars. Just messing around," he recalled in *Sporting News*. "When I started running Busch, I got serious. Everything about that was cool. Sure, I was seeking my father's approval. I wanted to make him proud. I'd been trying to do that all my life." Getting serious made all the difference for Earnhardt, who won the Busch series championships two years in a row, in 1998 and 1999. He won thirteen races during those two years, finishing in the top five in almost half the races he entered. When he entered the Busch series full-time, Earnhardt began driving a car owned by his father. In a fitting tribute to Ralph Earnhardt, who started the family racing dynasty, Earnhardt adopted his grandfather's number and has been racing in car number eight ever since.

Tragedy and triumph in racing's big leagues

For the 2000 season Earnhardt moved up to the Winston Cup circuit, NASCAR's most prestigious division. He quickly established his rookie season as one to remember, winning his twelfth race as well as his sixteenth. That season he also won the Winston, NASCAR's all-star race, becoming the first rookie to do so. He enjoyed a friendly rivalry with his father, who pushed his son toward success, not by easing off on him, but by riding him hard, just as he did every other racer in the field. Earnhardt entered his second season in the Winston Cup with high hopes, planning to build on his successes from his rookie year. He believed his chances were good to come up victorious in the Daytona 500 in February. On February 18, 2001, during the final lap of the Daytona 500, Earnhardt's father was involved in a serious

The Lowdown on NASCAR

NASCAR is among the most popular spectator sports in the world, and its popularity is growing. New fans may benefit from a "crash course" on racing to explain such things as the complicated system of point earnings, the various flags used in racing, and the origin of the term "stock car."

What does "stock car" mean? When NASCAR began in 1947, the stock cars came straight from the supply, or stock, of a car dealer, giving fans the notion that they, too, could start their engines and race to the finish line. NASCAR soon realized that regular street cars were not made to endure the tough conditions of racing, and driving teams were sneaking around the rules to make modifications anyway, so the rules were changed to allow for extensive customization of racing cars.

How fast can the NASCAR cars go? The available power of a typical NASCAR engine is around eight hundred horsepower. The cars are capable of speeds in excess of 230 miles per hour (mph), but recent NASCAR regulations require the installation of a restrictor plate between the carburetor and the engine. This plate minimizes the airflow into the engine and limits its power to about 450 horsepower. Even with the restrictor plates, NASCAR racers reach speeds approaching 200 mph.

How do the cars handle turns at such high speeds? Nextel Cup cars are fitted with a unique suspension spring, shock absorber, and alignment setting at each wheel to help them with turns. This construction allows the drivers to turn to the left with very little movement of the steering wheel. When not on a curve, however, drivers have to turn the wheel to the right in order to go straight.

What do the various flags used during races mean? The green flag starts the race or resumes it if there has been a caution period. The yellow flag signi-

---

multi-car crash. Earnhardt finished second in the race, but no celebrations followed. Dale Sr. was rushed to the hospital; it was determined later that he had died instantly from the crash. The Earnhardt family, as well as millions of devoted fans, were devastated.

All eyes were on Earnhardt in the aftermath of the crash; close friends observed that the young man seemed to grow up overnight, thrust into maturity by the loss of his father. Unable to grieve privately, Earnhardt and his family had to cope with the fans' sorrow as well as their own. One week later, Earnhardt returned to the driver's seat to race at the North Carolina Speedway. That race ended badly, as Earnhardt was slowed in the first lap by a minor accident. He struggled over the next couple of months, performing poorly in many of his races. In July he headed back to the site of his father's death, the Daytona International Speedway, for the Pepsi 400. His stepmother, Teresa, did not attend the race, unwilling to return so soon to that arena.

fies a problem on the track, including an accident, debris, or light rain. The caution situation usually lasts for at least three laps, during which drivers cannot pass the pace car. The white flag signifies that there is one lap remaining in the race; the black-and-white checkered flag means that the leading car has crossed the finish line, and the race is over. Other flags include the red flag, which signals that everything, from drivers to pit crews, must come to a halt. This flag appears at the start of a rain delay or in the case of a serious accident. A black flag waved at a particular car means that driver must return to the pit, perhaps because the car is emitting smoke or losing parts. The black flag with a white "X," shown to drivers who received the black flag but did not go to the pit, signifies that the driver is disqualified until he "pits." The blue flag with an orange diagonal stripe is an optional flag signaling drivers to use courtesy in situations when the leaders are approaching from behind and trying to get past.

What is pole position? This term refers to the number-one starting position. The driver who posts the fastest time during a qualifying round earns the pole position, giving him the best possible starting point for winning the race.

How do drivers earn points? The winner of each NASCAR race earns 180 points, with the second-place finisher earning 170. The point totals of those finishing in places three through six decrease by five-point increments; in other words, the third-place finisher will get 165 points, and number four will get 160. The points for positions seven through eleven go down in increments of four, and for positions twelve through forty-three, the points go down by threes. Bonus points are also available in each race, with drivers earning five points for every lap they lead and an additional five points going to the driver who led the most laps. When the Nextel Cup series gets close to the end of the season, the point totals are adjusted for the series leaders in what is called the "Chase for the Championship." At the end of the season, the driver with the most points is the Nextel Cup champion.

Earnhardt somehow put aside his grief, focused tightly on the track in front of him, and emerged victorious. "I will be crying sooner or later," Earnhardt said of his feelings for his father after the emotional victory, as quoted in the *NASCAR.com* profile of his family. "I dedicate this win to him—there ain't nobody else." Earnhardt went on to two more significant victories that season, winning at Dover, Delaware, in September, the first race after the terrorist attacks of September 11, 2001, and winning in October at Talladega, the site of his father's last first-place finish before his death. Earnhardt finished the 2001 season ranked eighth in points (racers are awarded a certain number of points for each race based on their finish), with nearly $6 million in winnings.

While Earnhardt had a mediocre season on the tracks in 2002, his popularity soared. *Sports Illustrated*'s Jeff MacGregor speculated on the phenomenal adoration of his fans: "Until the time of his

Dale Earnhardt Jr. sits in his race-car after winning the 2003 NASCAR Busch Series Aaron's 312. AP/Wide World Photo. Reproduced by permission.

father's death, Dale Jr. ... had inspired in fans only the kind of tentative, speculative affection that surrounds the son of any famous man....The fans' affections, their swarming passions, untethered after his father's accident, are beginning now to bear down on him." Conscious of his appeal to the masses, corporations beat a path to his door, offering millions of dollars in endorsement deals in return for Earnhardt plastering their logos all over his car and clothing. He published a book about his rookie Winston Cup season, *Driver #8,* which reached number four on the *New York Times* best-seller list and stayed on that list for seventeen weeks. He still mourned his father's loss—MacGregor quoted him as saying, "I used to miss him every minute. Now I've got it down to about every five minutes"—but he had begun to move on. He took on a much greater role in Dale Earnhardt Inc., the racing team begun by his father and owned by his stepmother, focusing on the team's long-term success.

During the 2003 season, Earnhardt performed better than he had in any prior year. He won two Cup races, at Talladega and Phoenix. He had thirteen top-five finishes, and finished in sixth through tenth place another eight times. His final Cup standing was third place, his highest finish since entering the Winston Cup division. He continued to win the fervent admiration of fans, who voted him NASCAR's most popular driver; he won more votes, 1.3 million, than the rest of the top-ten drivers combined. Earnhardt began the 2004 season with a flourish, winning the celebrated Daytona 500 on February 15, almost three years exactly after his father's death on the same track. Whether he goes on to have a career that matches his father's stellar performance or simply remains one of a handful of top NASCAR drivers does not seem to matter to his fans. After his Phoenix victory in late 2003, a reporter asked Earnhardt how things might change if he became a Winston Cup champion. Earnhardt considered the question, according to *AutoWeek* magazine, and responded, "I don't know if it would be a whole lot different. Fans cheer for you not because of wins, but … because of who you are, what you represent, and your attitude."

For More Information

Periodicals

Cavin, Curt. "The People's Choice." *AutoWeek* (November 10, 2003): p. 64.

Lambert, Pam. "Junior Achievement." *People* (March 8, 2004): p. 71.

MacGregor, Jeff. "Dale Earnhardt Jr. and NASCAR Nation." *Sports Illustrated* (July 1, 2002): p. 60.

McCarther, Mark. "Junior's Got a Brand New Bag." *Sporting News* (August 25, 2003): p. 20.

Spencer, Lee. "The Ties That Drive." *Sporting News* (August 6, 2001): p. 48.

Web Sites

"Dale Earnhardt Jr." *Dale Earnhardt Inc.* http://www.daleearnhardtinc.com/content/motorsports/t_driver.aspx?t=8 (accessed on June 27, 2004).

Dale Earnhardt Jr. http://www.dalejr.com/ (accessed on June 27, 2004).

Deitsch, Richard. "Their Finest Moments." *SI.com.* http://sportsillustrated.cnn.com/2004/racing/05/25/earnhardt_moments/index.html (accessed on June 27, 2004).

"The Earnhardts" and "Q&A: Dale Earnhardt Jr." *NASCAR.com.* http://www.nascar.com/ (accessed on June 27, 2004).

Hollingsworth, Joe. "NASCAR Explained." *Advance Auto Parts.* http://www.advanceautoparts.com/howtos_tips/automedia_html/pht/PHT200 30801WC/PHT20030801WC.htm (accessed on June 27, 2004).

Shirin Ebadi

1947 • Hamadan, Iran

Lawyer, human rights activist

Before October of 2003, most people outside of Iran—and many people inside that country—had never heard of Shirin Ebadi. She was not a major world leader, negotiating to end wars or topple repressive dictators. She was not a high-profile diplomat, traveling the globe and fighting against poverty or injustice. Ebadi was, and is, an Iranian Muslim lawyer who has devoted her life to improving the lives of victims of human rights abuses, particularly women and children in her home country. A human right is any right considered to belong to all people, including the rights to life and liberty, self-expression, and equality before the law. In recognition of her efforts, Ebadi was awarded the Nobel Peace Prize in December of 2003, a prestigious award given annually to a person or organization for extraordinary efforts on behalf of peace and social improvement. The first Muslim woman and the first Iranian citizen to earn this prize, Ebadi has since commanded a much wider audience for her speeches as she attempts to convince the world that Iran can be both a moderate democracy—a people whose leaders are fairly elected and responsible to the citizens—and a nation guided by Islamic values.

A voice for the silenced

Ebadi was born in Iran in 1947. Her father, Muhammad Ali Ebadi, was an important lawyer and law professor who contributed significantly to the writing of Iran's trade laws. Ebadi chose to follow in her father's footsteps, training to be a lawyer at the University of Tehran. During the 1970s she supported the reforms of Iran's leader, Mohammad Reza Shah Pahlavi, referred to simply as the shah, as he worked

....

"I sound like a dreamer, I know. The challenge facing us today is to think like dreamers but act in a pragmatic manner. Let us remember that many of humanity's accomplishments began as a dream."

to increase the rights of women and to reduce the powers of the nation's Muslim religious leaders. In 1975 Ebadi became the first woman judge in Iran. She held the position of president of the city court of Tehran, the capital city of Iran, until 1979. She married Javad Tavassolian, and they have two daughters who were born in the 1980s.

After the revolution of 1979, which deposed the shah and instated a conservative Islamic government, women were no longer allowed to have such important jobs, and Ebadi was forced to give up her position. The leader of Iran after the revolution was Ruhollah Musawi Khomeini, a conservative religious leader who had risen through the ranks of Islamic teaching to achieve the honored title of "ayatollah." He derived broad support from the lower-level clergy, known as mullahs, who advocate strict application of Islamic law to all aspects of Iranian life. Ebadi had initially supported the idea of the revolution, believing it would improve conditions in Iran. After the ayatollah took over, however, he created an atmosphere of suspicion and fear, enforcing religious regulations with brutality and intimidation. He immediately reversed most of the shah's social reforms, tightly restricting the rights of Iranian citizens, particularly women. Ebadi realized that she, and millions of others, had been deceived about the ayatollah's intentions.

Unlike many of her fellow intellectuals—teachers, scientists, artists—she chose to stay in Iran during a difficult period when anyone suspected of disagreeing with the Islamic state could be arrested, imprisoned, and tortured. Her decision to stay and fight for change while keeping within the bounds of the law earned her the respect of many in her country. Prevented by government decree, as all Iranian women lawyers were, from practicing law on her own, she joined an all-male law practice during the 1980s and began working on human-rights cases. Under the ayatollah's repressive government, which enforced its laws by inflicting violence on and withholding basic rights from the people, Ebadi had plenty of battles to fight. During her years as a judge, she had seen numerous cases that illustrated the unfair treatment of women and children in Iran. Ebadi dedicated herself to changing such laws and to acting as the voice of those who were silenced by the government.

The long road to reform

After the death of the ayatollah in 1989, some of the restrictions imposed by the religious leaders were eased. Women were again allowed to practice law, and Ebadi struck out on her own. She sought justice for those whose rights had been violated by the government, often providing her legal services for free. One of her notable cases involved the murder of a nine-year-old girl by her father. Despite the fact that the father was a proven drug abuser who had prevented his daughter from attending school, the father had gained custody of her when the parents divorced. The laws overwhelmingly favored fathers in custody battles, and those same laws allowed the father to avoid any jail time after he killed his daughter, claiming that fathers have the right to do what they choose with the lives of their children. Ebadi took on the case to help the mother find a measure of justice. She argued that the custody laws were grossly unfair and that the father

A Recent History of Iran

Beginning in 1941, Iran was led by Mohammad Reza Shah Pahlavi, known simply as "the shah." In some respects, the shah ruled Iran harshly, forbidding other political parties to form and tightly controlling the press. However, he also instituted a number of social changes, including placing a greater emphasis on secular, or nonreligious, education rather than on religious schooling and giving more rights to women than they had had under previous leaders. Most of his reforms proved controversial with the country's religious leaders, who claimed that giving more freedoms to women went against Islamic values. They opposed any reforms that reduced their own power. One influential religious leader, Ruhollah Musawi Khomeini, an ayatollah (a high-ranking religious leader) and a philosophy professor at an Islamic religious school, or *madrasah,* sharply criticized the shah's policies. The government responded by raiding the school, killing several students, and arresting Khomeini.

Khomeini was sent into exile, living for several years in other countries of the region, including Iraq and Turkey; he later lived in France. During his exile he kept in close contact with his followers in Iran, promoting the notion of a takeover in Iran that would change the leadership from secular to strictly religious. Meanwhile, during the 1970s, Iran encountered numerous economic hardships, and discontent spread. Even those who had at one time supported the reforms of the shah began to believe that it would be best for the country if he were overthrown. In January of 1978, numerous followers of the Ayatollah Khomeini held demonstrations, joined by many others who were frustrated by the lack of jobs and rising prices. The shah's government responded harshly to these demonstrations, and a number of protesters were killed. These deaths only fueled the rebellion, however, as each protester killed by the government was championed as a martyr, a hero who had died for the cause. The demonstrators demanded that the shah step down. In January of 1979, after a year of

should be punished for the murder. While her victory was small—the father was given just a one-year prison sentence—it was also significant, as she managed to change the custody laws so that fathers abusing drugs or inhibiting their children's education would not be able to obtain custody. This change in the law came too late for the nine-year-old girl, but it undoubtedly helped other children.

In addition to her work as a lawyer, Ebadi has also worked as a lecturer at the University of Tehran and has written a number of books on the subject of human rights, including *The Rights of a Child: A Study of Legal Aspects of Children's Rights in Iran* and *History and Documentation of Human Rights in Iran*. Ebadi has helped found several groups that work to promote human rights in her country, including the Association for Support of Children's Rights in Iran and the Center for the Defense of Human Rights. She was one of 134 people who signed the 1994 Declaration of Iranian Writers, a pro-democracy

violent protests and brutal crackdowns, the shah and his family fled Iran.

Khomeini returned to Iran on February 1, and by April 1, after a nationwide referendum—a special election—Iran was declared an Islamic state, with Khomeini as its leader. While the takeover had been accomplished with the support of numerous groups aside from the religious leaders, once Khomeini took power, the clerics excluded their former partners from all important posts in the government. All social reforms, including those that had established nonreligious schools and that had relaxed restrictions for women, were revoked. Khomeini and his followers instituted strict religious rules, which were violently enforced. In the years of the shah's rule, Iran had developed close ties with the United States, and its culture had become increasingly westernized—that is, displaying a resemblance to societies of North America and Western Europe. After Khomeini took over, the government sought to destroy all traces of westernization in Iran. A group of protesters loyal to Khomeini took over the American embassy in the city of Tehran. They took sixty-six U.S. citizens hostage, demanding that the shah, who was then undergoing cancer treatments in the United States, be returned to Iran. The hostage crisis was eventually resolved; the shah did not return to Iran and died soon after in Cairo, Egypt.

A bitter war that would result in massive civilian deaths began when Iraq invaded Iran in September of 1980. During the war, after terrorist bombings originating from within Iran had killed numerous clerics and government leaders, Khomeini's followers responded with brutal attempts to squash any rebellion. They arrested suspected enemies of the state on the flimsiest evidence, and prisoners were often deprived of basic human rights: tortured, raped, and executed. The war with Iraq ended in July of 1988, and less than a year later, in June of 1989, Khomeini died. Following his death, a struggle for control of the country erupted among various groups, some wishing to maintain the strict social and religious culture of Khomeini's rule and some arguing for a loosening of religious regulations, broader rights for women, and the reestablishment of relations with the West, particularly the United States. Various other groups held positions between those two extremes.

letter to the government denouncing all forms of literary censorship. Ebadi applied her considerable energy to the campaign of moderate presidential candidate Mohammad Khatami, who was elected by an overwhelming majority in 1997 and reelected in 2001. In spite of Khatami's moderating influence, however, reforms since his election have been minimal due to the entrenched power of the country's religious leaders. In a nation where the legal system is based not on a constitution but on sharia law—Islamic law derived from the Koran, Islam's sacred writings—and where that law is interpreted by conservative religious leaders, reform-minded leaders fight an uphill battle.

Ebadi has not argued for abandoning sharia as Iran's legal basis, but she does believe that sharia can be interpreted differently than it has been traditionally, allowing for greater freedom and equality for all citizens. She has expressed repeatedly her belief that Islamic law and democracy can be compatible and that human rights are possible

Shirin Ebadi (right) receives the Nobel Peace Prize, December 10, 2003. Ebadi holds the Nobel Diploma and Ole Danbolt Mjos, chairman of the Norwegian Nobel Committee, holds the medal which goes along with the prize. AP/Wide World Photos. Reproduced by permission.

in Iran. In a 2003 article for the *Weekly Standard,* Ebadi told journalist Amir Taheri: "If the present regime does not reform and evolve into one that reflects the will of the people, it is going to fail, even if it adopts a secularist posture." In other words, to Ebadi, the most important element of government is that it be democratic, subject to the wishes of the general public, whether under a religious or nonreligious banner.

Recognized by Nobel

After many years of working to improve conditions for women and children in Iran, Ebadi's work began to attract international notice and recognition. She received the Rafto Prize from the Norwegian government in 2001 for her work promoting human rights and democracy. Two years later, to her great surprise, she was chosen by the Norwegian Nobel committee as the recipient of the 2003 Nobel Peace Prize. Ebadi won an amount equal to well over one million dollars, which she then donated to the organizations she leads in Iran. In the aftermath of winning the prize, Ebadi looked back on Iran's recent history in an article in *Europe Intelligence Wire:* "Compared to twenty-five years ago, I can only see progress. But in a lot of areas, freedoms are still restricted. Freedom and democracy are not handed to you on a silver platter. Neither are they achieved with American tanks."

In spite of the international attention she gained after receiving the Nobel Prize, Ebadi confessed in an article in London's *Sunday Times* that she still feared for her own safety: "Anyone who fights for human rights in Iran lives in fear. But I have learnt to overcome my fear. In Iran anything could happen to anyone. My fight is to make sure that only good things happen to my people." Various groups in Iran disagree with Ebadi over what those "good things" might be and over how to accomplish them. At one end of the political spectrum, many young Iranians want nothing short of radical change in their country: they want to change Iran from an Islamic state to a secular, democratic country. They feel that Ebadi is too willing to give in to the powerful mullahs, the religious leaders, and that she does not use her tremendous influence to effect significant change. Some women's groups also attack Ebadi for not being more critical of the religious leaders. They dismiss Ebadi's claims that the laws of Islam, if interpreted correctly, can be compatible with human rights and democracy; these groups believe the only way a woman can be truly free is to live in a secular society. Such activists call for a revolution, an overthrow, while Ebadi advocates an evolution, a gradual change. While liberal activists consider Ebadi too timid in her reform attempts, those at the other end of the spectrum, the hard-line religious clerics, consider her a dangerous radical. These clerics, or mullahs, oppose any suggestion that women and children be given more rights. They reject the notion of easing traditional Islamic laws and resist any attempt to reduce their own power and influence.

At many points throughout her career, Ebadi has paid a high price for her views and her actions. Investigating cases involving the deaths of Iranian intellectuals and reformers in 2000, Ebadi obtained evidence that some religious leaders and conservative politicians had been behind the murders. She was subsequently arrested and imprisoned for more than three weeks, held in solitary confinement. Ebadi has received numerous death threats, which increased by thirty times after she won the Nobel Prize. She has been attacked in Iranian newspapers and labeled a traitor. She was forced by protestors to stop giving a speech at Al-Zahra women's university in December of 2003. She has been criticized by some religious Muslims in Iran for not wearing the *hijab,* the traditional Muslim headscarf, when she travels abroad and for shaking hands with men during such travels. Ebadi responds to such attacks by coolly repeating that she believes in Islam as a religion of peace, justice, and democracy. She points out that the Koran contains numerous references to democratic ideals, such as respecting the ideas and opinions of others.

After winning the Nobel Prize, Ebadi received numerous invitations to speak in many different countries. Through her speeches and media coverage, Ebadi's work became known to millions. Details of her courageous battles for justice in Iran have inspired people all over the world, and Ebadi has made it clear that winning a prominent international prize has only confirmed her decision to fight for change in Iran. She also signaled that, regardless of her level of fame, she would not compromise her message or her beliefs. She openly criticized the United States for its war on terror and for its 2003 invasion of Iraq. In her speeches and writings she has emphasized the importance of education and social justice in the fight against terrorism, explaining that such violence can only be stopped by addressing the causes of terrorism. She has argued that if those inclined to commit acts of terrorism were offered the hope that their lives would improve—a chance to be lifted out of poverty and to benefit from a fair and just system—they would no longer feel the desperation that leads to such acts. In an article in *Newsweek International,* Ebadi expressed her wish that future generations will carry on the fight for reform, making greater strides than she has: "I hope that young Iranians can go further than me. My generation had very little means to keep itself informed. When I was young we had neither computers nor the Internet. Our only source of information was a small library at the university. So I hope that today's young people can do much more and do better for our country than I did."

For More Information

Periodicals

Dorsey, Gary. "Nobel Cause." *Baltimore Sun* (May 15, 2004).

"Ebadi to Give Nobel Prize Money to Rights Charities." *Europe Intelligence Wire* (December 9, 2003).

MacLeod, Scott. "Shirin Ebadi: For Islam and Humanity." *Time* (April 26, 2004): p. 118.

Sunday Times (London) (October 19, 2003).

Taheri, Amir. "Iran's First Lady." *Weekly Standard* (November 3, 2003).

Valla, Marie. "Shirin Ebadi." *Newsweek International* (October 20, 2003): p. 92.

"Women a Force for Change in Iran." *Europe Intelligence Wire* (March 8, 2004).

Web Sites

Ebadi, Shirin. "In the Name of the God of Creation and Wisdom." *Nobel e-Museum.* http://www.nobel.se/peace/laureates/2003/ebadi-lecture.html (accessed on August 1, 2004).

Michael Eisner

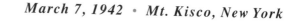

March 7, 1942 • Mt. Kisco, New York

CEO of Walt Disney Company

When Michael Eisner came on board as Disney's chairman of the board of directors and chief executive officer, or CEO, in 1984, many observers wondered if he could handle the business end of running an entertainment company. In his previous jobs as an executive at ABC and as president and CEO of Paramount Pictures, a major Hollywood film studio, Eisner had developed a reputation as a creative genius, an idea man. As the leader of the legendary Walt Disney Company, Eisner proved that he could balance creativity with sound business sense. He revitalized the company's animated films division, expanded and improved the Disney theme parks, acquired major television networks and cable stations, and made the Disney brand an almost universal presence, found everywhere from fast-food restaurants to toy stores to cruise ships.

In a 2000 interview with the *Harvard Business Review,* Eisner spoke of the need to weigh creative ideas against business demands, to create magic but at the same time keep within a strict budget. "In a creative person, just as in a creative company," he stated, "you have to have … a creative outlook and one that embodies common sense, side by side, inseparable. If you don't, then you get neither art nor commerce." After Eisner had spent nearly twenty years at Disney, many of the company's investors began to feel that he was no longer maintaining that delicate balance between art and business, and that he had sacrificed some of Disney's special qualities for the sake of improving profits. Eisner came under attack from many on Disney's board of directors as well as members of the public who owned stock in the company, and in early 2004, he was ousted as chairman of the board.

> "A leader, in my opinion, really has four roles. You've got to be an example. You've got to be there. You've got to be a nudge, which is another word for motivator, really. And you've got to show creative leadership—you have to be an idea generator, all the time, day and night."

He kept his position as CEO, but many in the industry wondered how long he could continue at the helm of Disney.

Starting at the bottom

Michael Dammann Eisner was born in Mt. Kisco, a small town north of New York City, in 1942. His father, Lester Eisner Jr., was a Harvard-educated lawyer and an investor in real estate, and the family was quite wealthy. Eisner's parents placed a strong emphasis on social graces—Eisner wore a sport jacket and tie at family dinners—as well as on education and culture. They encouraged their children to read often, and the family frequently attended the theater. Eisner's interest in theater continued during his years at Lawrenceville School, an expensive boarding school in New Jersey, where he was in a theatrical club and pursued acting. During his college years, at Denison University in Ohio, Eisner again found himself drawn to the theater. Deciding that he did not want to be an actor, he began writing plays, one of which was produced by the school's drama club. During the summer between his junior and senior years of college, Eisner had a job as a page, or assistant, at NBC, a job he obtained through his father's friendship with the television network's then CEO, Robert Sarnoff. The job was neither glamorous nor important, but it laid the foundation for Eisner's long and celebrated career in the entertainment industry.

After he graduated from Denison in 1964, Eisner returned to NBC, working as a Federal Communications Commission (FCC) logging clerk, keeping track of the times that commercials aired. He then moved to CBS, where he was responsible for placing commercials during children's programs as well as such shows as *The Ed Sullivan Show* and *Jeopardy.* Feeling restless and eager for a more important job in television, Eisner sent out hundreds of resumes. He received one reply, from a twenty-four-year-old executive at ABC named Barry Diller. Diller hired Eisner, and in the fall of 1966, Eisner began working for ABC, where he would spend a significant part of his career. The following year he married Jane Breckenridge, a computer programmer; they would go on to have three sons together.

Express lane to the top

Eisner rose quickly through the ranks at ABC, becoming the head of daytime and children's programming by 1971. He created two long-running soap operas during that time, *One Life to Live* and *All My Children,* as well as launching the cult-favorite educational series *Schoolhouse Rock.* During that time, ABC became the top-rated network on Saturday mornings, when their children's cartoons aired. As an executive developing prime-time shows a few years later, Eisner had a critical role in delivering the long-running hit show *Happy Days* as well as such 1970s classics as *Starsky and Hutch, Barney Miller,* and *Welcome Back, Kotter.* During his time at ABC, Eisner helped bring the network from its third-place ratings slump to the first-place position.

In the spring of 1976, Paramount Pictures, one of the major film studios in the United States, hired Eisner as president and CEO;

Walt Disney: The Man behind the Mouse House

Although Walt Disney died in 1966, his presence is still felt both within the walls of the Walt Disney Company and in the hearts of fans worldwide. He invented the concept of movie-length cartoons, in the process bringing to life such fairy tales as *Snow White and the Seven Dwarfs, Sleeping Beauty,* and *Cinderella.* He was also responsible for some of American popular culture's most enduring characters, including Mickey Mouse, Donald Duck, and Goofy. Disney established the theme parks Walt Disney World and Disneyland, which have endured as popular vacation destinations for tourists from all over the world.

Born in Chicago, Illinois, in 1901, Disney grew up on a farm in Missouri, later moving to Kansas City. He began drawing at a young age, incorporating into his creations the many animals on the family farm. He learned basic drawing skills from a course he completed by mail and from classes he took at local museums. After volunteering with the Red Cross during World War I, Disney began his career drawing illustrations and creating primitive animated cartoons for an advertising agency. He moved to Hollywood in 1923, with few possessions and no prospects. His brother, Roy, already living in California, supported Walt emotionally and financially, and the two set up shop together. With the new company struggling and desperate for a break, Walt developed a cartoon character named Mortimer Mouse; his wife, Lillian, suggested he change the name to Mickey, and thus, a legend was born.

Mickey Mouse's first appearance was in a 1928 cartoon short called *Steamboat Willie,* notable for being the first fully synchronized sound cartoon, meaning that the sound aligned with the actions of the characters. Walt Disney himself provided the voice of Mickey, with drawings by Ub Iwerks. Mickey Mouse was an immediate sensation, and the Disney company could stay afloat. Walt displayed a tireless drive for technical innovation, constantly seeking out ways to improve his cartoon shorts. He also proved to be a creative powerhouse, contributing his own ideas and shaping others' storylines as well.

Disney expanded his company's operations with the opening of a studio where a crew of animators could train and work. In 1937 Disney released *Snow White and the Seven Dwarfs,* the first feature-length cartoon. Taking several years and costing nearly $1.5 million to make—an unheard-of sum in those days—

his former coworker at ABC, Barry Diller, was chairman of Paramount's board of directors. Paramount was struggling at the time, in last place among the studios, but it took Eisner just two years to reverse the company's fortunes, bringing it to the top of the list. He distinguished himself there as a studio head who skillfully controlled costs while also contributing to the creative end of filmmaking, overseeing script development and other aspects of film production. Under Eisner's guidance, the studio released such hits as *Saturday Night Fever, Raiders of the Lost Ark, The Bad News Bears, Grease,* and *Beverly Hills Cop.*

Snow White retains its status as a film classic today. Disney followed the success of this film with other such animated classics as *Pinocchio, Dumbo,* and *Bambi.* Disney also achieved tremendous success with live-action family films, with his greatest success being the 1964 masterpiece *Mary Poppins.* In the mid-1950s, Disney began producing cartoons and live-action programs for television, including *The Mickey Mouse Club* and *Zorro.*

After attending an amusement park with his children, Disney began to dream of creating a Disney theme park that would appeal to children and adults alike. He opened Disneyland in Anaheim, California, in 1957. In just a decade, the park attracted nearly seven million visitors. Years later, Disney made plans for a second theme park in Orlando, Florida; Walt Disney World opened in 1971, five years after his death. His dream of developing a city of the future was realized in 1982 with the opening of the Epcot Center (Epcot stands for Experimental Prototype Community of Tomorrow).

In Disney's assessment, his greatest contribution to future generations was the establishment of the California Institute of the Arts, known as Cal Arts, a college-level school designed to train students in the visual and performing arts. In Disney's biography at the company's Web site, he is quoted as saying of Cal Arts, "It's the principal thing I hope to leave when

Walt Disney. The Library of Congress.

I move on to greener pastures. If I can help provide a place to develop the talent of the future, I think I will have accomplished something." As Disney fans will attest, his legacy goes far beyond Cal Arts. Disney has been described as a legend and a folk hero, and his name has become synonymous with the concepts of creativity, imagination, and enterprise.

Disney boss

In the fall of 1984, Eisner left Paramount to become the CEO of Disney at the request of founder Walt Disney's nephew, Roy Disney. At the time of Eisner's arrival at the Mouse House, the entertainment giant was struggling. Most of Disney's profits came from its theme parks, and even the parks were not doing as well as they once had. The company's films were not successful, and it did not have a strong presence on television. Eisner quickly set about to change Disney's fortunes, and he was tremendously successful: within less than twenty years, Eisner increased the company's annual revenues from less than $2 billion to more than $25 billion. He began by expanding Disney's television programming, approving the sale of old cartoons, films, and television shows to TV networks. He initiated substantial additions and improvements to the company's U.S. theme parks, Disneyland Resort in California and Walt Disney World in Florida. Eisner also approved the construction of two theme parks outside the United States, Euro Disney in France and Tokyo Disneyland in Japan. While Euro Disney initially performed relatively poorly, the Disney parks in the United States became far more successful than in years past. Disney even took to the seas, establishing the Disney Cruise Line with ships acting as floating miniature theme parks.

Disney saw huge profits once it began releasing videotapes—and later, DVDs—of its popular films and flooding the market with toys, clothing, and other products that tied in to the films. The natural next step was to open retail stores to sell these products, and the Disney Store became a staple at shopping malls all across the United States.

Under Eisner's leadership, Disney became a major player in television, purchasing Capital Cities, the company that owned Eisner's former employer, ABC, in 1996. Disney thus also became the owner of another Capital Cities property, the cable sports network ESPN. Disney also owns the cable networks Lifetime, E! Entertainment Television, and others. Eisner established the company's own cable network, the Disney Channel. With hit shows like *That's So Raven, Lizzie McGuire,* and *Kim Possible,* the Disney Channel has earned a huge following among kids of all ages.

During Eisner's years on the job, Disney also made a comeback in the film department, creating movies for adults as well as scoring new hits with their traditional animated fare for children. In addition to owning such film studios as Touchstone Pictures, Dimension Films, and Hollywood Pictures, Disney acquired the independent production company Miramax, which went on to create numerous critical and popular successes, including *Shakespeare in Love, Chicago,* and the *Spy Kids* series. For several years, it seemed Disney could not miss with its children's fare, releasing one animated smash after another: *The Little Mermaid* in 1989, *Beauty and the Beast* in 1991, *Aladdin* in 1992, and *The Lion King* in 1994. In the mid-1990s, animated films created on computers began to edge out the traditional two-dimensional animation of the Disney classics, but Eisner had ensured that Disney had a piece of that pie as well. Disney had formed a partnership with Pixar Animation Studios, the innovative company responsible for the computer-animated *Toy Story* movies, *A Bug's Life, Monster's Inc.,* and *Finding Nemo.* Disney found new life for its animated classics on the Broadway stage, achieving huge success with the theatrical versions of *Beauty and the Beast* and *The Lion King.*

Trouble in paradise

During 1994, Disney's president and Eisner's trusted partner, Frank Wells, died in a helicopter crash. In the years following, highly public battles between Eisner and such top Disney executives as Michael Ovitz and Jeffrey Katzenberg played out in the press. By the beginning of the twenty-first century, Disney was struggling on many fronts, returning to the pre-Eisner days of relying on the theme parks for a significant portion of its profits. After the terrorist attacks in New York City and Washington, D.C., on September 11, 2001, tourism fell off drastically, and even the theme parks' earnings began to dip.

During 2004, Disney's relationships with Pixar and Miramax soured. Pixar, demanding a greater share of earnings from the Pixar/Disney film partnership, refused to sign a new distribution contract with Disney and set about finding another partner. When Disney sought to prevent Miramax from distributing a politically charged documentary, *Fahrenheit 9/11,* by controversial filmmaker Michael Moore, Miramax's founders, Bob and Harvey Weinstein, found a way to sidestep parent company Disney for the film's distribution. The scuffle over *Fahrenheit 9/11* was just one in a series of disputes between Eisner and the Weinsteins, and speculation grew that Disney might be willing to sell Miramax.

Also during 2004, Eisner found himself doing battle with his company's board of directors, some of whom questioned whether he was the right man to lead Disney in the twenty-first century. Chief among his detractors was Roy Disney, nephew of Walt, the same man who had pushed for Eisner's hire back in 1984. Roy Disney, as well as many people who own Disney stock, had begun to feel that Eisner's aggressive selling strategies had robbed the company of much of its magic. Eisner's enthusiasm for "branding"—tirelessly promoting the Disney brand through the creation of sequels for nearly every Disney film or by emphasizing a film's product tie-ins as much as the film itself—had angered devoted Disney fans. At the annual shareholders' meeting in March 2004, thousands gathered to express their displeasure. Roy Disney spoke to the audience, summing up the feelings of many, as quoted in *Newsweek:* "Branding is something you do to cows. Branding is what you do when there's nothing original about your product. But there is something original about our products. Or at least there used to be." Applause erupted from the crowd. When it came time to vote, 43 percent of the shareholders refused to vote for Eisner's reelection to Disney's board of directors. This vote of no confidence resulted in his being removed as chairman. Eisner remained as the CEO, though many in the industry speculated that his grasp on the company had weakened and he would not remain at Disney for long.

When Disney encountered difficulties at the turn of the twenty-first century, Eisner expressed his confidence that the company would rebound. In an interview with the *Harvard Business Review,* Eisner stated that while Disney might occasionally miss the mark, the company has never lost the ability to entertain. Speaking of Disney's various theme parks, he told interviewer Suzy Wetlaufer: "If you look at people's faces, you'll see that Disney still knows how to sweep people off their feet, out of their busy or stress-filled lives, and into experiences filled with wonder and excitement. We sell fun and—not to sound arrogant, really just to sound proud—we still do that better than anyone." The problem, according to many investors and Disney insiders, is that Eisner places too much emphasis on the "sell" part of that formula, and not enough on the "fun." Whatever Eisner's future at Disney, few could argue that he has failed to leave his mark. In the years since he took over, Disney has gone from a beloved but struggling company to a media powerhouse with a significant presence in film, television, radio, publishing, and on the Internet—not to mention the more than seven hundred Disney stores and the hugely successful theme parks. Under Eisner's guidance, the company has gone far beyond Mickey Mouse and Snow White. Not every fan appreciates Eisner's influence on the company, but his powerful leadership style has ensured a lasting future for Disney.

For More Information

Books

Eisner, Michael, with Tony Schwartz. *Work in Progress*. New York: Random House, 1998.

Periodicals

Bart, Peter. "The Ultimate Survivor Mobilizes New Tactics." *Daily Variety* (March 15, 2004): p. 4.

"Eisner's Resume: A Rapid Rise." *Newsweek* (September 28, 1998): p. 54.

Jefferson, David J., and Johnnie L. Roberts. "The Magic Is Gone." *Newsweek* (March 15, 2004): p. 52.

Wetlaufer, Suzy. "Common Sense and Conflict: An Interview with Disney's Michael Eisner." *Harvard Business Review* (January 2000): p. 115.

Web Sites

"Michael D. Eisner." *Disney Online*. http://psc.disney.go.com/corporate/communications/bios/Eisner.html (accessed August 1, 2004).

"Walt Disney: A Biography." *Disney Online*. http://disney.go.com/vault/read/walt/index.html (accessed August 1, 2004).

Olafur Eliasson

1967 • Copenhagen, Denmark

Artist

Olafur Eliasson is not a traditional artist. His best-known works cannot be hung on a wall and do not involve paint or a camera or sculpting materials. Eliasson creates what is known as installation art. This unconventional modern art form can be described as art that viewers must walk through or around to experience. Installation art is usually created for a particular space, whether inside a museum or outside in a field, and for a particular period of time. It cannot be owned by collectors or museums: it exists for a time, and then it is taken down. It cannot be preserved for future generations, except through words and photographs.

Eliasson's works make use of natural elements, including light, water, fire, and wood, and he often combines these elements to re-create the outdoors inside, producing effects such as an indoor waterfall or rainbow. The artist has been displaying his works for the public since the mid-1990s, gaining an ever-larger following among art lovers. With *The Weather Project* (2003) Eliasson found his widest audience yet, capturing the imagination of millions. The exhibit opened in Turbine Hall of London's Tate Modern museum in October of 2003. In the first month alone, six hundred thousand visitors attended; by late December, that number swelled to one million. According to Sebastian Smee of the *Daily Telegraph,* Eliasson "has created some of the most exhilarating, thought-provoking, and vivid works of art anywhere in the world in recent years."

Northern light

Eliasson was born in Copenhagen, Denmark. He spent his childhood in Denmark, returning to Iceland, his parents' native country, for summers.

> **"I think there is often a discrepancy between the experience of seeing and the knowledge or expectation of what we are seeing."**

The stark northern landscape of his youth informed his artistic sensibilities, giving the artist a keen appreciation for what P. C. Smith of *Art in America* called "the changing drama of natural light." Eliasson attended the Royal Academy of Arts in Copenhagen from 1989 to 1995. At the academy, he studied the traditional ways of creating art—painting, sculpture, drawing—and learned about the old masters of the art world. During that time, he also turned his attention to the subject of human beings, researching neurology, the study of the nervous system, and Gestalt psychology, a way of analyzing human behavior and perception.

Eliasson's works include photography and sculpture, but he is best known for his installations. Beginning in the mid-1990s, he has participated in a number of exhibitions all over the world, with his works featured at such prominent museums as the Solomon R. Guggenheim Museum in New York, the Museum of Contemporary Art in Los Angeles, and London's Tate Modern. He has had a number of solo exhibitions, as well, at the Musée de l'Art Moderne de la Ville de Paris in France; at the ZKM (Center for Art and Media) in Karlsruhe, Germany; and at the Kunsthaus Bregenz in Austria. Eliasson represented Denmark in the 2003 Venice Biennale, a prestigious international art exhibition held every two years in Venice, Italy. The art exhibition is just one part of the Biennale, which conducts an array of annual events celebrating film, dance, architecture, music, and theater. Eliasson has made Germany his home base for much of his career, living in Cologne and later moving to Berlin.

Imperfect illusions

Many of Eliasson's works have the quality of an illusion, with the artist creating in an indoor space such natural phenomena as a foggy mist or the light of the sun. The artist takes care, however, that his illusions are not perfect. Eliasson always makes obvious the mechanism for producing the illusion: the water pump and punctured hose that create a misting effect, the electrical wiring that powers the lights of his "sun." In describing *Beauty,* an installation wherein Eliasson created an indoor rainbow, critic Daniel Birnbaum of *Artforum International* praised the artist's decision not to hide the tools he used for creating the effect: "There are no secrets, just a fascinating optical phenomenon to behold. Instead of being tempted to look for some veiled gadgetry, the viewer is thus confronted with the thing itself: the fact that light and water in combination produce color." By displaying his re-created natural elements in settings where such elements are not generally found—such as in a gallery or on a busy city street—Eliasson encourages audiences to reflect upon the relationship between the natural world and the urban world and between nature and human beings. Visitors seeing a foggy mist fill a room in a gallery experience that fog in quite a different way than if it were outside. Mary Sherman of the *Boston Herald* acknowledged that, even though it's obvious that an illusion is created by the artist, "our senses are heightened, our mind is sent racing, the world seems transformed, and, for a brief moment, the illusion is real."

For Eliasson's works, the audience always plays an important role, indicated in part by his tendency to use the possessive pronoun "your" in many of his titles. While the artist produces the work, its impact comes from the way audiences react. In 1996 Eliasson had his first New York City installation, *Your Strange Certainty Still Kept.* It featured an artificial waterfall constructed inside the gallery. Eliasson

James Turrell: Light Artist

Like Olafur Eliasson, James Turrell uses light and space as his tools for creating art rather than paintbrushes or a camera. Eliasson's works are often said to have been influenced by those of Turrell, who has been given many different labels, including environmental artist, land artist, and light artist. Like Eliasson, Turrell has studied both art and psychology, with a special interest in the subject of human perception, the way people interpret what they see or feel. His works explore the concept of light as an object, a physical material, not just something that illuminates other things. With such works as *Gard Blue* and *Danae,* Turrell created geometric sculptures out of light. At first glance, such sculptures appear to have a physical form, to be tangible, but a closer examination reveals that they are pure light.

Born May 6, 1943, in Los Angeles, California, Turrell has been exhibiting his works for the public since the late 1960s, with installations in important museums all over the world. He has won several prestigious prizes in the United States, including a MacArthur Foundation Fellowship, a grant from the National Endowment for the Arts, and a Guggenheim Fellowship, as well as earning numerous awards abroad.

The most significant work of his career is the *Roden Crater,* a project he began in the late 1970s and which has cost more than $10 million. The projected completion date for the *Roden Crater* has shifted in recent years, from 1999 to 2004 to some time around 2006. Created from an extinct cone-shaped volcanic crater in the Painted Desert near Flagstaff, Arizona, the *Roden Crater* consists of several tunnels and underground chambers with openings to the outside. At its base, it has a diameter of one mile, and the distance from the base to the rim is seven hundred feet. Work-

hung a rain gutter, punctured many times over, from the ceiling and pumped water to the gutter, which then rained down through the numerous holes. The falling droplets were lit by flashing strobe lights, creating the illusion that each drop was momentarily suspended in mid-air. *Your Sun Machine*, created in 1997, consisted of a bare room with a large circle cut out of the roof. Throughout the day—at least during sunny days—the sun shone in through the hole, its beams traveling across the wall as the day went on. The movement of the sun throughout the day constituted a major part of the work; another important aspect was the viewer's self-awareness, as described by the Web site of Tate Modern: "the viewer was reminded of his or her own position as an object, located on earth, spinning through space around the real sun."

Your Now Is My Surroundings, displayed in late 2000 in New York City, comprised two parts. The first was a small room, constructed of drywall, with a concrete floor. The glass had been removed from a skylight in the ceiling, occasionally resulting in rain collecting on the floor. Mirrors lined the walls from eye level up to the opening in the

ing with astronomers, Turrell has crafted an observatory of sorts, a way for people to observe the wonders of the sky and the play of natural light at various points of the day.

As Paul Trachtman explained in *Smithsonian*, "Some of the spaces are precisely, mathematically oriented to capture rare celestial events, while others are shaped and lit to make everyday sunsets and sunrises look extraordinary." Trachtman described his experience of witnessing a sunset from within one of the chambers, called the Crater's Eye, which has smooth white walls that slope toward the circular, open ceiling, making the room appear like "some cosmic egg." The way that Turrell has lit the interior of the Crater's Eye alters visitors' perceptions of the night sky above, as explained by Trachtman: "Strangely, as the colors deepen, the sky seems to drop down onto the crater. It loses its ordinary sense of being somewhere 'up there,' and ends up 'down here.'"

Turrell has gone to extraordinary lengths to make his vision of *Roden Crater* a reality. By the time it is completed, he will have spent something like thirty years devoted to this project. He joked to Trachtman that the price of the *Roden Crater* has had a human element as well as monetary, costing him "a couple of wives and several relationships." Turrell obtained grazing leases for many acres of land surrounding the crater and became a cattle rancher, in part as a source of income but primarily to prevent construction of new homes on the land, homes that would use artificial light and alter the sky at night. The time, effort, and money spent on the *Roden Crater* seem inconsequential, however, when Turrell's goals for the project are considered. He hopes it will survive for thousands of years, and he has planned with astronomers for the spaces within to wonderfully display celestial events predicted to take place far into the future.

ceiling, reflecting the sun, sky, and clouds. *Your Repetitive View,* part of the same exhibit, consisted of a thirty-three-foot-long wooden chute that extended through the gallery's interior walls, across a room, and straight through a window to the outside. Viewers could look through one square-shaped end to see the outdoors, a view that Eliasson had transformed from ordinary to "quite magical," as described by Eleanor Heartney in *Art in America:* "the interior of the shaft was lined with mirrors that seemed to draw in light and color from outside, and fracture them along its length." Frances Richard of *Artforum International* described the artist's exploration of seemingly opposite concepts in this installation: "interior and exterior, stability and reflection, architecture and emptiness." The tension between indoors and outdoors is a theme frequently found in Eliasson's works: the notion of escaping the bustle and confinement of a city, even when in the very midst of that city, through an encounter with the natural world. Heartney concluded that, with this installation, "the experience was startling, as the everyday world became a space as unfamiliar as it was mesmerizing."

Visitors at the Tate Modern Gallery in Longon, England, lie under Olafur Eliasson's The Weather Project. AP/Wide World Photos. Reproduced by permission.

While some of Eliasson's works might seem simple in the overall effect, they involve extensive calculations and preparations. Johanna Burton of *Artforum International* suggested that the artist's creative processes "are made up of equal parts architecture and science fiction and supplemented by a mammoth dose of advanced mathematics." Her suggestion is accurate: to help him with the planning and execution of his installations, Eliasson employs experts in a variety of fields, including architecture, carpentry, metalworking, engineering and structural design, and mathematics.

The Weather Project

The Weather Project, Eliasson's wildly popular 2003–2004 installation at London's Tate Modern, consisted primarily of the artist's version of the sun and sky. Upon walking into the massive hall, visitors saw a giant glowing disc suspended from the ceiling, an unmistakable representation of the sun. The light of this "sun" shone through a hazy mist, generated by humidifiers placed along the length of the hall. A glance at the ceiling revealed that it had been plastered with mirrors, reflecting the many visitors gathered far below. Upon closer examination, visitors could see that the "sun" was not actually circular; the artist had hung a half-circle of lights, which, when reflected in the mirrors on the ceiling, gave the impression of a complete circle. The hundreds of mirrors, applied in a jagged way rather than laying perfectly flat, gave the upper edges of the "sun" a rough, uneven appearance, making it look startlingly real. For those just entering the hall, the people already inside were silhouetted, appearing as dark figures against the bright yellow-orange light.

With *The Weather Project,* as with many of his works, Eliasson explored his views on the relationship between the natural world and the city. Regardless of how insulated a city dweller might be from nature, some aspects necessarily intrude, namely in the form of weather: rain, wind, sun, snow. With this installation, Eliasson created the illusion of nature and weather indoors, giving viewers a sense of the beauty and peacefulness of a sun-drenched mist. But he also allowed people to see the artificial nature of his creation. Those attending the installation could walk around the various parts of the installation, noting the electrical wiring powering the "sunlight" and the humidifiers creating the mist.

When asked by Fiona Maddocks of the *Evening Standard* what the work is about, Eliasson replied, "It's definitely first and foremost about people. People are looking at themselves as much as at art." The installation provoked unusual behavior among many visitors, behavior not ordinarily seen in museums. Visitors spent hours in Turbine Hall, sprawled on the floor, gazing up at the mirrors in an attempt to locate their reflections. Some even grouped together to create interesting shapes with their bodies that would be reflected above. Others had picnics on the gallery floor or sat in silent meditation. Maddocks reported that "there's much serious kissing." In the view of Richard Dorment of the *Daily Telegraph*, the reactions of the visitors added a layer of meaning and significance to the work: "What the artist began, the audience completes. It is the visitors that make *The Weather Project* unforgettable."

For More Information

Periodicals

Birnbaum, Daniel. "Olafur Eliasson." *Artforum International* (April 1998): p. 106.

Burton, Johanna. "Olafur Eliasson." *Artforum International* (September 2003): p. 224.

Dorment, Richard. "A Terrifying Beauty." *Daily Telegraph* (London, England) (November 12, 2003).

Heartney, Eleanor. "Olafur Eliasson at Bonakdar Jancou." *Art in America* (February 2001): p. 135.

Maddocks, Fiona. "The Weather Man." *Evening Standard* (London, England) (November 20, 2003).

Richard, Frances. "Olafur Eliasson." *Artforum International* (January 2001): p. 136.

Sherman, Mary. "Special Effects." *Boston Herald* (February 6, 2001).

Smee, Sebastian. "The Artist Who Paints with the Weather." *Daily Telegraph* (London, England) (September 30, 2003).

Smith, P. C. "Olafur Eliasson at Tanya Bonakdar." *Art in America* (December 1996): p. 92.

Trachtman, Paul. "James Turrell's Light Fantastic." *Smithsonian* (May 2003): p. 86.

Web Sites

Olafur Eliasson. http://www.olafureliasson.net/press/ (accessed August 1, 2004).

"Olafur Eliasson: The Weather Project." *Tate Modern*. http://www.tate.org.uk/modern/exhibitions/eliasson/eliasson.htm (accessed August 1, 2004).

Missy "Misdemeanor" Elliott

1971 • Portsmouth, Virginia

Hip-hop artist

Missy Elliott has accomplished the extraordinary. Hundreds of rap artists have made successful records, written hit songs, and produced other artists' work; some have even headed up their own record labels. Few of them, however, have been women. Rap is a male-dominated art form; the music is filled with aggressive, often violent, imagery and negative attitudes toward women. The chances of a young musician making it big in the music industry are slim in the best of circumstances, but for a woman to become hugely successful in the world of hip-hop is nothing short of phenomenal. Elliott has achieved success on her own terms: she writes, produces, and arranges her music; she controls the direction of each new album; and she has refused to play along with someone else's idea of what a female rapper's image should be. For Elliott, this strong-willed approach to her career has paid off. She has written and/or produced songs for Christina Aguilera, Justin Timberlake, Beyoncé Knowles, Whitney Houston, and Janet Jackson. She has released five of her own albums since 1997, and each has sold upwards of one million copies. She has forged an innovative, light-hearted, sexy style that trumpets her self-confidence and willingness to take a risk. In a review of her 2003 album, *This Is Not a Test!,* Rob Sheffield of *RollingStone.com* assessed her accomplishments: "After seven years at the top, she still sounds as hungry and driven as ever, refusing to repeat past successes, pushing on to newer and weirder realms while everyone else is catching up to what she was doing five years ago."

A rough start

Born Melissa Arnette Elliott in Portsmouth, Virginia, Elliott is an only child who experienced intense personal conflict as a child. Elliott was the victim of sexual abuse by an older cousin when she was eight

> **"**I don't have these lyrics where you be like, 'Wow.' But music is music, and as long as I make people want to dance, make them happy, then I don't really trip off of what other people say. I just do music.**"**

years old, and she frequently witnessed her father physically abusing her mother. She recalled to *Entertainment Weekly*'s Rob Brunner: "I never wanted to go stay at my friends' houses because I always thought my father would beat my mother up or kill her or something." In spite of such traumatic events, Elliott has recalled lighter moments as a music-obsessed youngster. She remembers shutting herself in her room and pretending to be a superstar singer. She told Kevin Chappell of *Ebony:* "When I was four, I used to sing to my doll babies. They had rotating arms, I used to lift them up and pretend that they were clapping for me." She had little interest in schoolwork, preferring instead to listen to music, imitate her musical heroes—like Michael Jackson—in the mirror, and write songs.

Longing for escape from her painful home life, Elliott wrote letters on a daily basis to Jackson and his sister, Janet, begging them to come to her school and take her back home with them. The Jacksons never came to her rescue, but one day, when Elliott was fourteen, her mother did: Patricia Elliott packed up their things, took her daughter, and left. "My mother leaving my father changed my life," Elliott told Chappell. "It made me a stronger person." The next few years proved difficult, with Elliott and her mother struggling to make it on their own. Elliott skipped school fairly often, but she stayed out of serious trouble. Continuing her fascination with music, she wrote song lyrics all over her bedroom walls. Her mother, initially upset, eventually gave in, as Elliott explained to Brunner: "My mother didn't want to fuss about too much. She just wanted me to be happy, because I'd been through so much.... [She] wanted to make sure that I was okay. She just was like, 'Okay, put another song up there. Who cares?'"

As a teenager, Elliott joined with three other girls to form a vocal group called Sista. She graduated from high school in 1990. The following year, after a concert by the R&B band Jodeci, Elliott and the other members of Sista approached Jodeci member DeVante Swing at a hotel. They performed a few songs for him, and Swing was so impressed that he signed them on to record for his production company. Sista recorded an album, but the group disbanded once the girls learned that the label, Elektra Records, was not prepared to release it. By that time Elliott had made several key connections in the recording industry. She formed a producing/songwriting team with her childhood friend Timbaland (1971–), with Elliott writing the songs and Timbaland producing the recordings. They contributed songs to the albums of numerous artists, including four singles on *One in a Million,* a CD by the late singer Aaliyah (1979–2001). Elliott also contributed vocals to other artists' tracks, including a fateful turn on Gina Thompson's 1996 song "The Things That You Do." Sylvia Rhone, chairman and chief executive officer (CEO) of Elektra Records, heard Elliott's contribution to the song and recognized a special quality about the guest singer. As Rhone told Brunner in *Entertainment Weekly,* "You just see it, you hear it, and you know that it says 'superstar.' It wasn't like we had to nurture or push. She could sing, she could rhyme, she could write, and she had a sense of what she wanted imagewise even back then." Rhone signed Elliott to a deal enabling

All about Eve

Like Missy Elliott, Eve Jihan Jeffers, better known to her fans simply as Eve, has defied convention with her career as a rapper. Through a combination of talent, luck, and determination, Eve has reached superstar status in a field where women have a hard time being taken seriously.

Born on November 10, 1978, Eve grew up in the low-income housing projects of Philadelphia, Pennsylvania. She knew she wanted to be a performer from an early age and joined an all-girl singing group with some friends. At age thirteen she decided she wanted to be a rapper, and she performed at local talent shows whenever possible. After graduating from high school, Eve met the influential rapper/producer Dr. Dre (1965–), who signed her to a record deal with his label After-

math. She moved to California for a time, working on writing and recording, but when the label dropped her, she returned to Philadelphia. She met rapper DMX, who introduced her to the Ruff Ryders, a group of rappers and producers in New York. Impressed by her spontaneous audition, the Ruff Ryders invited Eve to be their first female member. After an intense period of writing and rapping with the Ruff Ryders—what she called "boot camp" in a *Newsweek* article—Eve appeared on the group's successful compilation CD *Ryde or Die Vol. 1.* She also scored high-profile guest spots on songs with the Roots and with Blackstreet.

Her success with others prompted Eve to break out on her own, and she released her first solo album, *Let There Be Eve ... Ruff Ryders' First Lady,* in 1999.

---

her to write and produce songs. Elliott eventually had a contract to create her own album and to run her own record label, Gold Mind.

Streets paved with platinum

In 1997 Missy "Misdemeanor" Elliott, the budding rap star, released her debut album, *Supa Dupa Fly,* with guest spots by rappers Busta Rhymes, Lil' Kim, and Da Brat. Looking back on the album a few years later, Steve Huey of *All Music Guide* proclaimed that *Supa Dupa Fly* was "arguably the most influential album ever released by a female hip-hop artist." With Timbaland contributing his innovative producing skills, Elliott created a CD that crossed back and forth between genres, as expressed in a review at *RollingStone.com:* "The production ... marries hip-hop beats and succulent R&B with a cool, uncluttered glaze that flatters the rhythms instead of flattening them." Elliott showcased her versatility on this album as on those that followed, cowriting songs, singing, and rapping in her distinctive low-key, humorous style. Driven by the success of the single "The Rain

While the album bore the stamp of its Ruff Ryder producers, it also proudly displayed Eve's personality. Eve was not afraid to be sexy and feminine, but, unlike many of her fellow female hip-hoppers, she relied more on her talent than on her appearance to sell records. As explained by Lorraine Ali of *Newsweek,* Eve plays "as tough as the boys, but with a stealthy female elegance. She walks the fine line between the empowering, old-school style of Queen Latifah and the trashy titillation of Lil' Kim." The album debuted at number one on the *Billboard* 200 album chart—an extraordinary accomplishment for a female rapper—and sold two million copies.

Eve followed up her debut with *Scorpion* in 2001. While critics had mixed reactions to the album, her fans snapped it up. The single "Let Me Blow Ya Mind," a duet with No Doubt's Gwen Stefani, was a huge success, winning an MTV Video Music Award in 2001 and a Grammy Award in 2002. On her third album, 2002's *Eve-olution,* Eve branched out, singing rather than rapping on several tracks. She cited reggae and rock as influences on that album, expressing a distaste for the emphasis on drugs and violence in rap.

Eve showed fans another side of herself when she appeared in the Vin Diesel action movie *XXX* and in fellow rapper Ice Cube's *Barbershop* in 2002. She later earned her own sitcom on UPN, a show called *Eve,* which stars the rapper as a fashion designer looking for love. While critics dismissed the show, fans felt otherwise, and the ratings for the first season were solid. Eve juggled her music career, television show, and additional movies, returning for the sequel *Barbershop 2* and filming *The Woodsman* with Kevin Bacon and a comedy called *The Cookout,* all 2004 releases. Eve has also become famous for her fashion sense, and in the fall of 2003 she rolled out her own line of women's sportswear called Fetish.

(Supa Dupa Fly)," the album earned a nomination for a Grammy Award and found a huge audience as well, earning platinum certification by the Recording Industry Association of America (RIAA) for sales of at least one million units.

Elliott followed up her successful debut with *Da Real World* in 1999, an album boasting such hit singles as "She's a B***h" and "Hot Boyz." On the former track Elliott expresses her frustration that men can stand up for themselves and be respected while women who behave in assertive ways are described in nasty terms. In the song, she redefines the word in the title to refer to a strong woman. During 2000 Elliott spent less time in the studio and more time focusing on the work of new artists whose albums would be released on her Gold Mind label. She returned in 2001 with the release of *Miss E...So Addictive,* which includes the breakout singles "Get Ur Freak On" and "Scream a.k.a. Itchin'," both of which earned Elliott Grammy Awards for best female solo rap performance. The album features guest performances by a number of high-profile R&B and rap artists, including Jay-Z, Ludacris, Eve, Redman and Method Man, and Ginuwine.

In late 2001, Elliott paid a visit to her doctor, who told her she had high blood pressure. He advised that, if she wanted to live long enough to achieve all of her goals and enjoy her wealth into retirement age, she had better lose weight. Elliott, then thirty years old, took his advice to heart and began a strict regimen of eating healthy, low-sodium foods, drinking plenty of water, and exercising. Elliott began working out up to four times a day, using the treadmill, kickboxing, and lifting weights. After a few months, she had lost more than seventy pounds and lowered her blood pressure. Her physical transformation, as well as her continuously evolving musical style, are referred to in the title of her 2002 album *Under Construction*. Featuring the hits "Work It" and "Gossip Folks," the album is a nostalgic take on old-school rap, paying tribute to and sampling groundbreaking tracks of the genre. Elliott explained the thinking behind the album to Brunner in *Entertainment Weekly:* "For the new generation, it's gonna sound like something new. For the old generation, it's gonna be a memory. It works both ways." The album, achieving double platinum status with sales of over two million copies, impressed both fans and critics, including Gavin Edwards of *RollingStone.com,* who stated in his review of *Under Construction:* "It's hard to remember what the world was like before Missy 'Misdemeanor' Elliott came along, but historical records indicate that it was a lot more boring." Elliott went on to win her third Grammy Award in the category of best female rap solo performance for "Work It."

Missy Elliott kisses her 2004 Best Female Solo Performance Grammy Award. AP/Wide World Photos. Reproduced by permission.

Elliott released her fifth album, *This Is Not a Test!,* in late 2003. In keeping with her other albums, Elliott showcases the work of several high-powered guests, including Mary J. Blige, Jay-Z, R. Kelly, Nelly, and Beenie Man. Some critics described the album as containing too much filler and too few groundbreaking Elliott/Timbaland collaborations, but others, while acknowledging the release is less than perfect, suggest that even a flawed album by Missy Elliott stands above those of most of the hip-hop crowd. Sheffield concluded his review of this CD at *RollingStone.com* by saying, "Why anybody would choose to spend their life without a copy of *This Is Not a Test!* is a mystery."

The fruits of her labor

During 2004 the television network UPN announced the development of a reality series called *The Missy Elliott Project,* which would air in the middle of the 2004–2005 season. Executive produced by and starring Elliott, the show will feature a crew of aspiring hip-hop artists competing against each other in such categories as singing, rapping, and dancing. Elliott will help choose the winner, who will be offered a record deal with her Gold Mind label.

Known for her individualistic fashion sense, Elliott has added to her substantial earnings by endorsing such products as Sprite, Gap corduroy jeans—in commercials with pop superstar Madonna—and Adidas athletic wear. In 2004 she signed with Adidas to create her own line of athletic gear, called Respect M.E. (both a motto and a play on her initials), which includes sneakers, track suits, T-shirts, and hooded sweatshirts. Elliott does not exactly hide the abundant wealth she has attained from such deals as well as from sales of her albums and concert tickets. She possesses several residences, including a home in New Jersey, a lavish condominium near Miami, and a mansion built for her mother in Virginia Beach. Her car collection includes a Ferrari, a Lamborghini, and a Hummer. While Elliott acknowledges the pleasures of being rich, she also speaks often of how thankful she is for the life she leads and of how important it is for musicians to invest their money wisely rather than blowing it all on an outlandish lifestyle. She has displayed her desire to make a difference in the world by becoming the spokesperson for Break the Cycle, a national nonprofit organization dedicated to helping young people avoid abusive relationships and counseling those who have been victims of domestic violence. In all that she has done, Elliott has displayed an unwavering sense of self. As she told Chappell, "I'm not a follower. I'm not a copycat. I'm an original."

For More Information

Periodicals

Ali, Lorraine. "Diamond in the Ruff." *Newsweek* (March 12, 2001): p. 70.

Brunner, Rob. "Missy Elliott." *Entertainment Weekly* (November 22, 2002): p. 32.

Chappell, Kevin. "Eve and Missy Elliott: Taking Rap to a Whole New Level." *Ebony* (August 2001): p. 68.

Lynch, Jason. "Missy Universe." *People* (January 20, 2003): p. 77.

Web Sites

"The Complete Missy Elliott." *RollingStone.com.* http://www.rollingstone. com/?searchtype+RSArtist&query+missy%20elliott (accessed August 1, 2004).

"Missy Elliott." *All Music Guide.* http://www.allmusic.com (accessed on June 7, 2004).

Deborah Estrin

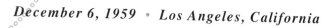

December 6, 1959 • *Los Angeles, California*

Computer scientist

Deborah Estrin is a pioneer in the development of a revolutionary technology called embedded networked sensing, or ENS. ENS involves the use of tiny, acutely sensitive monitoring devices that can "read" their surroundings, picking up extremely detailed information. When networked together—in other words, when the sensors can communicate with each other—and when embedded, or planted, in a particular environment, these sensors can not only pick up information, but they can also analyze and relay it back to scientists. If planted in a bridge or a building, sensors might convey information about the structure's soundness, pinpointing any weak areas that need reinforcement. Sensors embedded in a forest might gather information about the amount of water and nutrients in the soil as well as the eating habits of nearby wildlife.

Named as one of the "Brilliant 10" in *Popular Science* magazine's list of elite researchers, Estrin is the director of the Center for Embedded Networked Sensing (CENS) as well as a professor of computer science at the University of California at Los Angeles (UCLA). Her involvement in ENS has put her at the forefront of a burgeoning technology that could radically transform society. Just as the Internet connects a virtual world of computers and databases, a vast network of embedded sensing devices could serve as a communications system for the physical world, connecting streams of information about waterways, air, plant life, the animal kingdom, human-made structures, and far more. The full potential of ENS has yet to be completely explored.

A life of learning

Born in Los Angeles in 1959, Estrin was raised in a household that placed a premium on learning. Her parents, Thelma and Gerald, were

> "Estrin ... wants to connect us to the physical world as intimately as the Internet connects us to one another."
>
> **Laurie Goldman, *Popular Science*, September 1, 2003**

professors in the computer science department at UCLA, and both earned PhDs in electrical engineering. This was a notable accomplishment particularly for Estrin's mother, since relatively few women earned PhDs during the early 1950s, especially in scientific fields. "I was very fortunate," Estrin related in an interview with *U•X•L Newsmakers,* "to be surrounded by academics and role models, and to have a professional mother and a feminist father." She went on to explain that she and her two sisters, Judy and Margo, knew that their parents valued "education, career, having an impact in the world, [and] intellectual growth." All three girls took those values to heart; in addition to Estrin and her groundbreaking research and university teaching, Judy is a successful entrepreneur, while Margo is an accomplished physician specializing in internal medicine. Estrin's own intellectual curiosity has been passed on to the next generation as well: her teenaged son, Joshua, is interested in physics and nanoscience, the study of the world on a molecular or atomic scale.

From the time of middle school, Estrin focused intently on her studies, concentrating especially on science and technology. She also loved math, studying the subject at an advanced level from the seventh grade on. She knew as a child that she wanted to invent things. After graduating from University High School in West Los Angeles, Estrin earned a bachelor of science degree from the University of California at Berkeley in 1980. She went on to earn a master's degree in technology policy from the Massachussetts Institute of Technology (MIT) in 1982. Three years later, Estrin completed the PhD program in computer science at MIT.

After graduating from MIT, Estrin headed back to the West Coast to begin her teaching career. During 1986 she accepted a position as professor of computer science at the University of Southern California (USC), where she taught and conducted research until 2000. In 1987 she won the Presidential Young Investigator Award from the National Science Foundation (NSF), for her research on computer networking and security issues. From the late 1980s to the late 1990s, Estrin focused her research on designing network and routing protocols for large global networks like the Internet, essentially exploring the ways information is transmitted over a massive network of computers.

Special sensors

In the late 1990s Estrin turned her attention to the field of embedded networked sensing, and began to explore some of the possibilities for such devices. At the heart of an ENS device is a microprocessor that is about the size of a die-cast toy car such as those made by Hot Wheels. A microprocessor is at the core of any number of high-tech devices, from computers and cars to cellular phones and digital music players. The ENS microprocessors are combined with collections of various sensors. These might include a device to detect sound or motion or to determine chemical composition, or perhaps a video or infrared camera that can capture images that are outside the spectrum of colors visible to the human eye, such as body heat. The microprocessor, in effect, translates the information picked up by the sensor and allows scientists to make sense of it. These wireless sensing devices, when spread over a large area, can transmit information to the scientists monitoring them and, perhaps more significantly, can be instructed to send information only when a specified event of interest occurs.

Embedded networked sensors could have a multitude of uses. Food manufacturers might use them to monitor shipments of their products, determining their location and making sure they are being kept at the proper temperature. The potential applications in the medical field are numerous, including a sensor-embedded bandage that might signal doctors that a patient is developing an infection. Sensors embedded throughout an airplane might identify possible structural problems that could be fixed before the plane ever leaves the ground. At a 2002 seminar at the University of California at San Diego, Estrin suggested some of the possibilities of ENS to her audience. The Web site of the California Institute for Telecommunications and Information Technology quoted from Estrin's lecture: "Imagine high-rise buildings in downtown Los Angeles that could detect their structural faults, then alert authorities on corrective action.... What if buoys along the coast could alert surfers, swimmers, and fishermen to dangerous levels of bacteria?"

Deborah Estrin, holding up a sensor node. Courtesy of UCLA Today. © The Regents of the University of California.

Inspiration in a rain forest

During 1999 Estrin vacationed in Costa Rica, home to lush tropical rain forests. She was awed by the abundant animal and plant life in the rain forests and by the admirable focus of the Costa Rican government and people on preserving their country's biodiversity. Estrin realized that biologists could radically improve their ability to observe complex biological phenomena by using embedded networked sensors. Upon returning from Costa Rica, Estrin began to focus on the impact ENS could have on the study of biology, the environment, and other natural sciences. Among many other uses, ENS could help scientists track and monitor the impact of climate change on endangered ecosystems—a community of organisms and the surrounding environment—and could provide detailed information about the type and level of contamination in the soil or air. In 2000 Estrin left USC to become a professor of computer science at UCLA. As with all scientific endeavors, Estrin's research in the field of ENS depended on funding to carry it from the planning stages to actual testing of the sensing devices in the real world. Soon after joining the faculty at UCLA, she and several colleagues from UCLA, USC, and other universities began working on a massive grant proposal that would give them the funding they needed.

During August of 2002, Estrin and her colleagues heard the news they had anxiously awaited for many months, news of a grant the likes of which most scientists can only dream of: the National Science Foundation (NSF)'s Science and Technology Center awarded them a ten-year, $40 million grant to develop ENS technologies for the study of physical and biological systems. The grant allowed for the establishment of the Center for Embedded Networked Sensing (CENS), and Estrin was named the center's first director. Based at UCLA, CENS was one of six academic research centers to receive the 2002 NSF grant, which specifies that the work must be collaborative, involving people from various fields of study. Estrin's center includes professors from a number of different departments at UCLA and other universities, including computer science, electrical engineering, biology, and education. In exchange for the grant money, the research centers must commit to conducting their primary research, and to advancing educational opportunities in local schools and universities and increasing the number of minorities participating in the research. They must also connect with other research institutions as well as the business world and the surrounding community. CENS was ready and able to fulfill the many requirements, and work soon began on developing the initial programs for testing ENS technology.

Ecosystems and beyond

One year later, in August of 2003, Estrin and CENS began their first large-scale study of an ecosystem in the James Reserve, a protected area in the San Jacinto Mountains of southern California. The study will eventually deploy approximately one hundred sensing devices embedded over a thirty-acre wooded area. As Laurie Goldman summarized in *Popular Science,* "video cameras will watch bluebird nests, motion detectors will sense predators, and buried CO_2 probes will monitor soil chemistry." The study will focus on the impact of short-term changes in the microclimate—the climate of a small area—on plants and animals. The sensors will be set to detect such things as the movement of water through the soil and the growth patterns of various types of plants and trees. The ENS devices are also being used to track the feeding and reproduction habits of several species of birds in the area. In keeping with their commitment to make the data they gather accessible to the public, the scientists at CENS arranged for the results of the study to be available on the Internet at www.jamesreserve.edu.

Estrin and her colleagues have also experimented with embedding sensors in buildings and other human-made structures to gather information about earthquakes. These sensors can detect seismic, or earthquake-related, activity, and can measure the impact of such activity on a building, indicating strengths and weaknesses. Scientists hope that in the future such sensors could help prevent a building's collapse during a disaster. Seismologists, scientists who study earthquakes and related activity, know that during a strong earthquake in Mexico City in 1985, a number of skyscrapers collapsed because they were vibrating exactly in tune with the earthquake. In the long term, embedded networked sensors have the potential to structurally alter a building, essentially "detuning" it, giving it a better shot at surviving an earth-shaking disaster. Another early project headed by Estrin has involved the use of sensing devices for soil sampling in order to measure contaminant levels. Sensors could also be used to measure water contamination from industrial waste or other sources, zeroing in on the source of the problem in order to resolve it efficiently. In the world's oceans and coastal waterways, sensors could detect the presence of harmful microorganisms, like certain types of algae or bacteria, before the damage from such organisms becomes too great.

Ultimately, as Estrin described to *Newsfactor Innovation,* she envisions ENS as an ever-present technology: "In the long term, embedded networked sensing systems are likely to be in the car you drive to work; in the roads, embankments and traffic lights by which you drive; in the parking structures; in complex environments like hospital rooms; as well as outpatient monitoring setups in the home." To establish and then maintain so many sensory networks will require the cooperation of experts in a number of fields, from computer science and engineering to mathematicians, biologists, and information scientists. Estrin has recognized the importance of involving social scientists, legal experts, and others who can explore the potential impact on society of such in-depth monitoring. The widespread use of sensors in the future could raise important issues of privacy, such as sensors that might enable governments or other institutions to gather detailed information about the lives of private citizens. While a great deal of research and testing must take place before the full potential of ENS can be explored, Estrin has a notion of the technology's nearly limitless possibilities, and her role in the realization of those possibilities is a critical one.

For More Information

Periodicals

Fulford, Benjamin. "Sensors Gone Wild." *Forbes* (October 28, 2002).

Goldman, Laurie. "Deborah Estrin." *Popular Science* (September 1, 2003): p. 84.

Huang, Gregory T. "Casting the Wireless Sensor Net." *Technology Review* (July 1, 2003): p. 50.

Mervis, Jeffrey. "Research Centers: Science with an Agenda." *Science* (July 26, 2002).

Web Sites

"Biography." *Center for Embedded Networked Sensing.* http://www.cens. ucla.edu/Estrin/index.shtml (accessed on August 2, 2004).

Hamilton, Michael. "Making Sense of Nature." *James Reserve.* http:// www.jamesreserve.edu/news.html (accessed on August 2, 2004).

McDonough, Brian. "Networked Computer Sensors Infiltrate Everything." *Newsfactor Innovation.* http://sci.newsfactor.com/perl/story/18088. html (accessed on August 2, 2004).

"New Center for Embedded Networked Sensing Will Use Wireless Technology to Create Wide Array of Sensor Systems to Monitor Environment, Buildings." *UCLA News.* http://newsroom.ucla.edu/page.asp? menu=fullsearchresults&id=3246 (accessed on August 2, 2004).

"UCSD-TV and SD Telecom Council Team on New Program about Telecommunications." *California Institute for Telecommunications and Information Technology.* http://www.calit2.net/news/2002/10-25-estrin. html (accessed on June 21, 2004).

Other

Additional information for this profile was obtained from a personal interview with *U•X•L Newsmakers* (August 3, 2004).

Tina Fey

May 18, 1970 · *Upper Darby, Pennsylvania*

Television writer, screenwriter, actress

Tina Fey might have single-handedly made it hip to wear glasses in the mid-2000s, but there is more to the writer-actress-comedian than her trademark black-rimmed specs. In 1999 she broke into the boy's club by becoming the first female head writer on the long-running television comedy *Saturday Night Live* (SNL). In 2000 she proved she could deliver lines with the same dry wit after she stepped in front of the cameras to coanchor the popular SNL segment "Weekend Update." In 2004 Fey combined both talents when she wrote the screenplay and costarred in the teen comedy *Mean Girls.* Along the way, Fey also showed the world that smart is sexy: she was named one of *People* magazine's 50 Most Beautiful People of 2003.

A happy-go-lucky nerd

Tina Fey came from a family that appreciated humor. Born on May 18, 1970, in Upper Darby, Pennsylvania, she admitted to Associated

Press writer Douglas Rowe that her ultra dry wit comes from her mother, Jeanne. Fey also gives credit to her father, Don, and big brother, Peter, for introducing her to classic comedy. Some of her early memories are of watching comedies on television with her family, especially episodes of the British series, *Monty Python's Flying Circus*. Peter, who is eight years older, also gave Fey her first glimpse into the world of *Saturday Night Live*. SNL aired at 11:30 at night, and since Fey was too young to stay up and watch it, Peter would act out the skits for her the next day.

By the eighth grade, Fey was writing reports on comedy. She also carved out a role for herself as the class comedian. As Fey told

> **"Women tend toward more character-based, subtle observations. Men are more amused by fighting bears, sharks, and robots."**

Donna Freydkin of *USA Today,* she started to crack jokes in middle school, and when people laughed, she decided then and there, "this is going to be my thing. I'm going to try to be that person at the party." However, there was also a quiet side to the budding comedian. At Upper Darby High School, Fey was a serious student; she was very studious, and was involved in such activities as tennis, newspaper, choir, and drama. She was not particularly popular. In Fey's own words to Rowe, she was a "happy-go-lucky nerd who operated in my own little social situations outside of the cool people."

After high school Fey enrolled at the University of Virginia, intending to study English. She soon switched her major to drama, and when she graduated, Fey and a college friend took off to study acting in Chicago. Chicago was Fey's destination because it was the home of Second City, a famous training center for actors and comedians. The star-struck girl from Pennsylvania had grown up idolizing those actors on *Saturday Night Live* who had gotten their start at Second City—actors such as Gilda Radner (1946–1989), John Belushi (1949–1982), and Dan Aykroyd (1952–).

Queen Bees and Wannabees

Rosalind Wiseman's book *Queen Bees and Wannabees: Helping Your Daughter Survive Cliques, Gossip, Boyfriends and Other Realities of Adolescence* has become a best seller and is being recommended as an important book that gives parents a very realistic look at the world of teenage girls. As Wiseman tells parents, the social cliques of high school have become more complicated, and teenagers are so influenced by these groups that it can lead to extremely harmful behavior. Bullying can lead to violence; peer pressure can push kids into taking drugs or becoming sexually active.

Wiseman creates a navigation guide for parents, explaining the various kinds of social roles young girls take on. For example, there is the Queen Bee (the leader), the Sidekick, the Banker (a girl who uses secrets to move up in the group), and of course, the Target (the person who is singled out for harassment). She also outlines parenting techniques, offering advice on how to talk to teens and always suggesting that parents remember what it was like to be young and facing so many pressures. Taking the lid off "girl world" is often not pretty (the girls are, as the movie title says, mean), but Wiseman does try to inject some humor into her survival manual.

By the time she wrote the book, Wiseman was an expert on teens. She had spent more than a decade talking to thousands of young girls about cliques, problems with boys, issues with school, and, in general, how they felt about themselves. In 1992 she founded a nonprofit organization, called The Empower Program, to teach girls self-defense as a way of protecting themselves against violence. Since then the program has grown, and the organization offers strategies for use in schools that will help both girls and boys understand how to be more compassionate and how to become empowered enough to take a stand and stop violence.

Moves to *Saturday Night*

By day Fey worked the front desk at the local YMCA; at night she took classes at Second City, where as she told William Booth of the *Washington Post*, she became "completely addicted" to improv. Improv, short for improvisation, is a type of comedy in which actors perform together without a script. They spontaneously make up (or improvise) material as they go along, usually focusing on a particular theme or subject. According to Fey, improv made her a far better actor than her classical training in college, and everything clicked into place. As she explained to Booth, improv "tapped into the writer part of my brain and the actor part all at the same time."

After two years at Second City, Fey was asked to join the company's touring group, and in 1994 she was promoted to the Second City main stage in Chicago. The dedicated comedian appeared in eight shows a week for over two years. Although it was an exhausting period in Fey's life, it was also productive, and she managed to hone her skills as a writer, as well as a performer. In 1997 she took a chance and sent a few of her scripts to a Second City colleague who had gotten a job at *Saturday Night Live*. The producers liked what they read, and offered Fey a position on the writing staff. Fey jumped at the offer and moved to New York. Within a few weeks, her first sketch aired. Just two years later, in 1999, Fey was promoted to head writer—the first woman to hold the position in the twenty-seven-year history of SNL.

Saturday Night Live premiered on NBC on October 11, 1975, as an experiment. The concept was to showcase up-and-coming young comedians who might be too outrageous or too sophisticated for regular prime-time television. Hence, the cast became known as the Not Ready for Prime-Time Players. The ninety-minute live show aired at 11:30 P.M. on Saturday night and quickly developed a dedicated audience. In the 1970s millions of people stopped everything on Saturday night and gathered around the TV to watch their favorite skits and performers. In addition, the show gained such an important reputation, that to appear on SNL was an honor. The coolest music groups, the hottest stars, and the hippest comedians vied to take the SNL stage.

Injects some girl power

Over the years, however, SNL suffered from ups and downs as producers and writers changed, and cast members left to pursue Hollywood careers. By the time Fey took over the head writer's chair, the show was, as Booth put it, "faintly mildewy." From 1999 until the mid-2000s, SNL's ratings began to steadily rise, and in 2002 the writing staff took home an Emmy (the highest award given for excellence in television) for the first time in several years. Many people, including critics and fellow cast members, chalked up the show's comeback to Fey. As comedian Janeane Garofalo (1964–) explained to *People* magazine, "SNL has risen from the ashes again to be a very good show—in no small part thanks to Tina Fey."

Fey was also credited with bringing some major girl power back to the show. When she joined SNL, she was one of only three women on the twenty-two-member writing staff. As a result, one of the complaints was that female SNL players were not featured as regularly as the male performers. Fey changed all that. She created sketches that featured women and made it a point to showcase some of her old friends from Second City who had joined the cast, including Rachel Dratch and Amy Poehler.

In 2000 Fey became a featured player herself when she paired with fellow SNL-cast mate Jimmy Fallon (1974–) to cohost "Weekend Update," the one segment of the show that remained constant since the show's early days. Although the anchors changed from season to season, the point of the segment remained the same—to take current news and add a special bite of SNL commentary. Fey, the first woman to host the segment since 1982, added her own brand of wit and soon became known for her scathing observations, her low-key delivery, and of course, her trademark blue jacket and black glasses. She was a darling of the critics, and gained even more power on the show.

The Queen Bee of *Mean Girls*

By 2002, just five years after joining the show, Fey was helping *Saturday Night Live's* longtime producer Lorne Michaels (1944–) decide which sketches to put on the air and what players to feature. When Fey approached Michaels with an idea that could expand into a screenplay, he was all ears. While flipping through the *New York Times Magazine,* Fey was intrigued by a review of a book by Rosalind Wiseman, called *Queen Bees and Wannabees: Helping Your Daughter Survive Cliques, Gossip, Boyfriends and Other Realities of Adolescence* (2002).The book was a guide to help parents understand the potentially difficult world that teen girls find themselves coping with on a daily basis.

Fey believed that the book, although a work of nonfiction, had real movie potential. "What struck me the most," Fey said on the *Mean Girls* Web site, "were the anecdotes of the girls that were interviewed for the book. Rosalind, rightfully, takes them very seriously, but in my opinion, they're also very funny. I mean the way girls mess with each other is very clever and intricate." When she got the green light from Michaels, Fey started her research. The thirty-two-year-old pored through teen magazines and Web sites, and watched one teen movie after another. Of course, she also worked with Wiseman, promising her that she would not, as Fey told Booth, "turn it into a … stupid, cheesy teen comedy." Fey worked on the script for almost two years, sandwiching it in during her breaks from SNL. The result was the 2004 comedy *Mean Girls.*

Mean Girls focuses on seventeen-year-old Cady Heron, who grew up in the wilds of Africa and was homeschooled by her research scientist parents. When the family moves back to the United States, Cady finds out that life is harder in the high school jungle, where kids run in packs, and every day is a struggle to survive. She is caught between such cliques as the social outcast Mathletes and the ultra-popular, but ultra-malicious and much-feared leaders of North Shore High School, the Plastics. When Cady falls for hunky jock Aaron Samuels, who just happens to be the ex-boyfriend of the school's Queen Bee, Regina George, the Plastics go after the new girl with a vengeance. To retaliate, Cady, along with "art freaks" Janis and Damian, do some plotting of their own.

Tina Fey (left) poses with Lindsay Lohan, the star of **Mean Girls.** AP/Wide World Photos. Reproduced by permission.

Fey handled every rewrite of the script, which is unusual for a first-time screenwriter. She was also given a lot of control over the movie by director Mark Waters, who immediately signed on to the project after reading Fey's screenplay. As he explained on the *Mean Girls* Web site, "It was witty and funny and full of humor yet still had a kind of humanity to it that you could connect to." Moviegoers of all ages flocked to the May 2004 premiere, and it was number-one at the box office after its opening weekend. Critics praised Fey's "wickedly funny" writing and her ability to create characters and dialogue that rang true to life. As Cady might put it, Fey really tapped into "girl world."

A look behind the glasses

So, just how much of Tina Fey is in *Mean Girls*? According to the screenwriter, there is a little bit of her in several of the characters. She was boy-crazy like Cady, and although Fey told Freydkin, "Regina is an amalgam of girls I was intimidated by in high school," there is also a smidge of Fey in Regina as well. As she admitted to Booth, "I was a really snarky girl." Fey also appeared in the movie. She plays math teacher Mrs. Norbury, who at the movie's end, lectures the school's female student population that "Calling somebody else fat will not make you any thinner. Calling somebody stupid will not make you any smarter."

At home, the comedian is much more of an introvert and not at all like the characters she plays each week on *Saturday Night Live*. As her husband, Jeff Richmond, told Freydkin, "Her persona is so caustic, but she's very shy and she doesn't like confrontation in real life." Richmond is the musical director of SNL, and on Sunday, the couple's one day off from work, they enjoy lounging at home and baking desserts. The rest of the time, Fey is busy. She told *Entertainment Weekly* that she plans to stay with SNL "as long as they will have me," but she is also at work developing a sitcom for NBC. Will she star in it? Maybe. As Fey explained to Freydkin, "I like being a writer who performs."

For More Information

Books

Wiseman, Rosalind. *Queen Bees and Wannabees: Helping Your Daughter Survive Cliques, Gossip, Boyfriends and Other Realities of Adolescence*. New York: Crown, 2002.

Periodicals

Booth, William. "Tina Fey, Specs Symbol." *Washington Post* (April 25, 2004): p. N01.

"Girls' Night? With Tina Fey at SNL's Helm, a Former Player Sees Improvement." *People Weekly* (December 10, 2001): p. 19.

Meadows, Susannah. "Ladies of the Night." *Newsweek* (April 8, 2002): p. 54.

Schwartz, Missy. "The Smartest Girl in the Class." *Entertainment Weekly* (May 7, 2004): p. 32.

Schwarzbaum, Lisa. "Clique Magnet: Lindsay Lohan Is the Prey in the High School Jungle of Tina Fey's Sharp, Sassy *Mean Girls*." *Entertainment Weekly* (May 7, 2004): p. 57.

Smith, Kyle, and Brenda Rodriguez. "Leap of Fey: Saturday Night Live's Tina Fey Brings Her Specs Appeal to the Big Screen in *Mean Girls*." *People Weekly* (May 3, 2004): p. 75.

Web Sites

The Empower Program Web site. http://www.empowered.org (accessed on June 27, 2004).

Freydkin, Donna. "Fey Gets Her Skewers Out." *USA Today* (April 22, 2004) http://www.usatoday.com/life/movies/news/2004-04-22-fey-main_x.htm (accessed on June 27, 2004).

Mean Girls Web site. http://www.meangirlsmovie.com/indexflash.html (accessed on June 27, 2004).

Rowe, Douglas J. "SNL's Tina Fey Makes Screenwriting Debut." *FoxNews. com: Foxlife* (April 29, 2004) http://www.foxnews.com/story/0,2933, 118710,00.html (accessed on June 27, 2004).

Volume numbers are in italic; ***boldface*** *indicates main entries and their page numbers; (ill.) following a page number indicates an illustration on the page.*

C

h

i

◉

℗

Russert, Tim, *4:* 671
Rutan, Burt, *4:* **647–54,** 647 (ill.)
Rutan, Richard, *4:* 647, 650
Rutan Aircraft Factory, *4:* 649–50
Ryan, Leslie, *1:* 12
Ryan, Meg, *2:* 333
Ryan, Suzanne, *4:* 656, 657, 661
"Ryan Seacrest for the Ride Home" (radio show),
   4: 676
Ryde or Die Vol. 1, 1: 192
Ryder, Winona, *1:* 119; *4:* 740
Rylant, Cynthia, *2:* 370

S

Sackler, Howard
   The Great White Hope, 1: 10
Sacramento Kings (basketball team), *2:* 354
Safeco Classic (golf), *4:* 723
Safety (Coldplay), *1:* 111
Saget, Bob, *3:* 520
Sainden, Eric, *2:* 341
Salerno, Heather, *1:* 55, 56
Salesians (Catholic priests), *1:* 24, 27
Salinger, J. D.
   Catcher in the Rye, 3: 489
Salkind, Michael, *1:* 37
Salt N' Pepa, *2:* 214
Same-sex marriages, *3:* 497, 501–3, 502 (ill.)
Samoa, *2:* 376
Sampras, Pete, *3:* 633
Samsung World Championship of Golf, *4:* 722
Samuels, Allison, *2:* 214; *3:* 529
Samway, Patrick, *1:* 29
San Antonio Spurs (basketball team), *1:* 74
San Diego Chargers, *3:* 632
San Francisco
   same-sex marriages in, *3:* 497–503
San Francisoco 49ers (football team), *1:* 62
San Jose Earthquakes (soccer team), *1:* 7
Sanchez, Ricardo, *2:* 327
Sandalow, Marc, *3:* 576
Sandman (comic book series), *2:* 237, 240–43
Sandman: Endless Nights (Gaiman), *2:* 237,
   242–43

Sandman: Preludes and Nocturnes (Gaiman), *2:*
   242
Sandman: The Dream Hunters (Gaiman), *2:* 242
Sandman: The Wake (Gaiman), *2:* 242
Santa Claus Lane, 1: 148
Santa Monica Alternative Schoolhouse (SMASH),
   4: 752
Saris, *2:* 248–49, 255; *3:* 514, 515, 518
Sarnoff, Robert, *1:* 173
SARS. *See* Severe acute respiratory syndrome
Saturday Night Fever, 1: 174
Saturday Night Live, 1: *35, 36, 135;* 2: *380, 421;*
   3: *635;* 4: *739, 773*
      women writers for, *1:* 205, 206, 208–9, 211
Saved by the Bell: The New Class, 4: 778
Savile Row (London), *2:* 430
Savings and loan crisis (1980s), *3:* 563
"Say My Name," *2:* 404
SBC Communications, *4:* 688
Scaled Composites Inc., *4:* 651
Scalia, Antonin, *3:* 592
Scary Movie 3, 1: 11
Schaefer, Stephen, *3:* 600
Schilling, Mary Kaye, *1:* 115
Schmidt, Eric, *3:* 539
Schneider, Bill, *2:* 256
Scholastic Press, *2:* 232
School of Rock, 1: 33, 38–39
School violence
   empowering students against, *1:* 207
Schoolhouse Rock, 1: 173
Schorow, Stephanie, *1:* 129
Schrag, Daniel, *4:* 765
Schulberg, Bud, *4:* 743
Schultz, Michael, *4:* 701
Schure, Alexander, *2:* 360
Schwartz, Frederic, *2:* 416
Schwartz, Josh, *4:* **655–61,** 655 (ill.)
Schwartz, Stephen, *4:* 656
Schwartzman, Jason, *1:* 119
Schwarz, Alan, *4:* 645
Schwarzbaum, Lisa, *1:* 48; *4:* 743
Schwarzenegger, Arnold, *2:* 375; *3:* 502, 503; *4:*
   663–72, 663 (ill.), 665 (ill.), 668 (ill.)
Science
   inventions, *2:* 393–400
   paleoclimatology, *4:* 759–66

Yahoo!, *4:* 681–89
Yale Corporation, *3:* 518
Yang, Jerry, *4:* 684–85, 685 (ill.), 686
Yao Ming, *4:* **821–28,** 821 (ill.), 825 (ill.)
Yao Zhiyuan, *4:* 821
Yarbrough, Marti, *3:* 532
Yeager, Chuck, *4:* 649
Yeager, Jeana, *4:* 650
"Yellow" (Coldplay), *1:* 113
Yeshiva, *3:* 453
"You Don't Know Jack" (computer game), *1:* 52
Young, Kristin, *3:* 437
Young, Neil, *4:* 752
Young, Steve, *1:* 62
Young adult literature, *2:* 367–73; *3:* 483, 485, 486–89, 491, 493–96, 505–11; *4:* 733
Young Landlords, The (Myers), *3:* 487
Your Now Is My Surroundings (Eliasson), *1:* 184–85
Your Repetitive View (Eliasson), *1:* 185
Your Strange Certainty Still Kept (Eliasson), *1:* 183

Your Sun Machine (Eliasson), *1:* 184
You're a Good Man, Charlie Brown (play), *4:* 656
Y Tu Mama Tambtén, 3: 603
Yudkowitz, Marty, *3:* 611

Zaleski, Jeff, *2:* 243, 291
Zapatero, José Luis Rodríguez, *4:* **829–35,** 829 (ill.), 834 (ill.)
Zel (Napoli), *3:* 491, 493, 495
Zellweger, Rene, *4:* 796
Zemeckis, Robert, *2:* 343
Zhang Guojun, *4:* 827
Zhizhi, Wang, *4:* 824
ZKM (Germany), *1:* 182–83
Zoetrope (film company), *1:* 121
Zoglin, Richard, *3:* 617
Zombie movies, *2:* 342–43
Zoolander, 1: 35; *4:* 737, 739, 742, 743
Zorro (television show), *1:* 175